Margit Koemeda-Lutz, Helen Resneck-Sannes,
Maê Nascimento (Eds.)
Bioenergetic Analysis

Margit Koemeda-Lutz, Helen Resneck-Sannes,
Maê Nascimento (Eds.)

Bioenergetic Analysis

The Clinical Journal of the International Institute for Bioenergetic Analysis (2005), Volume 15

Psychosozial-Verlag

Bibliographic information of Die Deutsche Bibliothek (The German Library)
Die Deutsche Bibliothek lists this publication in the Deutsche Nationalbibliografie (German National Bibliography). Detailed bibliographical data can be accessed via internet (http://dnb.d-nb.de).

Original edition

E-mail: info@psychosozial-verlag.de
www.psychosozial-verlag.de

Cover: Jonathas Sousa de Medeiros: »Vibrant Body«, 2003
Cover layout: Christof Röhl
Draft design: Atelier Warminski, Büdingen
Editorial staff: Kristine Klein
Layout: Katharina Appel
ISBN 978-3-89806-395-1

Contents

Editorial

About one and a half years ago John Conger announced that he wished to resign as Editor-in-Chief of *Bioenergetic Analysis – The Clinical Journal of the IIBA* after eight years. In fall of 2003 I was appointed to be the new editor.

Since *Bioenergetic Analysis* is an international journal it was clear that an editorial board for it should comprise representatives from different continents and countries. Helen Resneck-Sannes from Santa Cruz, California, and Mae Nascimento from Sao Paolo, Brazil, fortunately were ready to join.

What is new is that we found a well-reputed publishing house, the *Psychosozial-Verlag*, Giessen, FRG, to produce our Journal and that we introduced a system of blind peer reviews for submitted manuscripts.

This issue contains three key note lectures from the IIBA conference 2003 at Salvador Bahia, Brazil (H.Resneck-Sannes, B.Lewis, H.Traue), two original articles (M.Nascimento and, A.Klopstech) and a review of Lowen's autobiography (P.Helfaer).

Bioenergetic Analysis is presently published once a year. We do hope that it continues to serve its purpose of being a medium of communication for the International Bioenergetic Community and of presenting our theoretical concepts and positions, our clinical expertise and psychotherapeutic skills to the wider scientific community.

The opinions and theoretical positions of the articles published in *Bioenergetic Analysis* are those of the authors. They do not necessarily represent the opinion of the editors or an official position of the IIBA. Thanks to our new review system we hope that they are skillfully written, scientifically well informed and sufficiently sophisticated so they will instigate serious dispute among our colleagues in the IIBA and from other schools of thought.

Helen, Mae and I have become a miraculous team during this past year, considering the fact that we live on three different continents, speak three different languages, never met in person and had no conference calls. E-mailing was our only means of communication.

This year has also provided insight into John Congers work during the past years. We admire it and would like to thank him on behalf of our professional community at this point in time.

We would also like to invite everyone in the membership of the IIBA to contribute to a continuously prosperous development of this journal whatever you have to offer.

I hope you all enjoy reading this issue!

Zürich, 1.12.2004
Margit Koemeda

Reviewers for this issue were:
David Finlay, Eugene
Margit Koemeda, Zürich
Myron Koltuv, New York
Bob Lewis, New York
Mae Nascimento, Sao Paolo
Helen Resneck-Sannes, Santa Cruz
Christa Ventling, Basel

Thank you very much for the time you spent!

Volunteers to be asked for reviews were:
Bea Amstutz, lic.phil., CH
Thomas Fellmann, Dr.med., CH
Daniel Bouko-Levy, M.D., FR
Ulrich Sollmann, Dipl.Soz., FRG
Anja van der Schrieck, Dr., FRG
Scott Baum, Ph.D., USA
Peter Fernald, Ph.D., USA
Angela Klopstech, Ph.D., USA

The Anatomy of Empathy[1]

Robert Lewis

I. Introduction

Today my topic is »the Anatomy of Empathy«. I will use the masculine pronoun in this paper for purposes of simplicity. We will look at our traditional Bioenergetic model and more recent developments as they bear on empathy. Although my title implies that the science of empathy has evolved to the point where I can draw you a map of the muscles and synapses that are involved, I will conclude that even with exciting recent advances, being empathic is still very much a clinical art. State of the art brain imaging confirms that the right brain is mediator of empathy, but does not yet help us to better intervene clinically. The behavioral anatomy data of facial expression, gaze behavior, vocal rhythm coordination and body posture is more immediately relevant to our topic. So empathy is complex. In this paper, building on the insights of Lyons-Ruth (1998), Stern (1985), Tronick (1989), Beebe and Lachmann (2002) and many others (Sander 1977, Weiss 1970 Fogel 1993), I will distinguish between explicit and implicit knowing, in order to better comprehend empathy. We will look at the limits to our explicit knowing, and the extent to which the implicit can be made explicit. I will also argue that a non-linear, dyadic systems view best captures the split second, bidirectional quality of empathic communication. Finally, I will touch on the paradox that the very wound which has led us to become therapists, both attunes us to our patients and interferes with our truly being with them. I will attempt to illustrate the above issues with clinical vignettes.

---

[1] Morning Lecture given on October 11, 2003 at the XVII th IIBA conference in Salvador Bahia Brasil.

II. Definitions

A) *Empathy*: The word empathy is derived from the Greek »empatheia«, meaning affection or passion. The Webster's new World College Dictionary (fourth edition) defines empathy as: »The projection of one's own personality into the personality of another in order to understand the person better; ability to share in another's emotions, thoughts or feeling.« Some therapists, Tansey and Burke (1989), for instance, embrace a broad definition; we are being empathic, they say, when we respond to the patient's need, when we give him what he needs in order to get better – even if that means failing him (so that he can re-experience and master his internalized traumas); we are responding empathically, when we receive the patient's projective identifications – projections that shape our experience as they deepen our understanding of the patient. For others, Stark (1999), for instance, this more inclusive definition obscures a crucial distinction between, on the one hand, the empathically positioned therapist who responds to something inside the patient's awareness – something that is experience-near and, on the other hand, the relationally confronting therapist who responds to something outside the patient's awareness.

But I do not want to discourage you so early in my talk ... perhaps later. Most of you might agree that while empathy is not easy to define, you know it when you experience it, you know what it feels like when you are in its presence ... is this true for you? ... I ask because a colleague told me of a recent study which suggested that the perception of empathy was just as effective as the real thing! This might bring to mind a colleague, with whom some of you are familiar, who commanded good fees because his patients perceived honesty and sincerity in his clear blue eyes. His fees climbed even higher as his hair turned gray and his patients perceived wisdom in his graying locks. And then finally, his sessions became priceless when he developed hemorrhoids and, as he sat with his patients, they perceived him as truly feeling their pain.

One last definition, one that feels right to me from Peter Kramer (1989) of Prozac fame: He says, »I became that part of me that was closest to him [his patient]« (p.138). If we think about what Kramer describes, (repeat the phrase) it makes sense that being empathic is a somewhat different process for each of us. There probably is a common neurobiology in our right orbitofrontal cortex that allows us all to amplify the resonant chord in us that is struck by our patient's experience. But we are so complex and unique, that the part, for instance, of ten different therapists, the resonant cord that is, which would be closest to a particular given patient, would be felt by some therapists in their guts, by others in their heart, etc. Some therapists would be fairly comfortable with the feeling, others would struggle to tolerate it, and so on.

B) *Implicit/explicit*: I believe it will help us to grasp empathic phenomena if we distinguish between the explicit and implicit modes of knowing. They rely on different neuroanatomic pathways and are defined as follows (Beebe and Lachmann, 2002): Implicit memory refers both to emotional and procedural memory, which are outside of awareness. The first two years of our lives are lived on a largely implicit level, which is why we usually have limited explicit recall for them. Procedural memory includes non-symbolically encoded action sequences which guide behavior (i.e., how to ride a bicycle). Explicit memory, as I am sure you will remember, is intentional recall of symbolically organized information and events.

C) *Dyadic, nonlinear, systems view of therapy*: My talk today is based on this view of therapy and empathic process. In it each member of the dyad is seen as simultaneously regulating both itself and the interaction. As Jaffe et al. (2001) put it: »At the nonverbal level of action-sequences, at every instant, any action in a dyadic relationship is jointly defined by the behavior of both partners.« Finally, Fogel (1993) tells us that in a systems model, »all behavior is simultaneously unfolding in the individual, while at the same time each is modifying and being modified by the changing behavior of the partner«. An example would be a young child that is too aroused by a mother's facial approach and who then looks away and/or touches himself to self-regulate his level of arousal. The child has simultaneously both soothed himself and sent a message to his partner. Research has shown that parents are well-attuned or empathic only twenty to thirty per cent of the time. But securely attached children have parents that within two seconds at the most, being themselves secure and well-attuned, can allow the child the space and freedom to down-regulate both them (the parent) and the interaction. The interaction has been »repaired« (Tronick,

1989). Research has shown that this same implicit, nonverbal split-second dyadic regulatory system operates throughout the life cycle.

III. Remember that we have the bioenergetic tools, but never forget that we ourselves are the instruments

Bioenergetic Analysis has traditionally said that we have the tools to see a person's story engraved in the form and motility of their body. This was one of Wilhelm Reich's (1933, 1945) original and profound contributions. One could spend years debating how much of a person's story we can see in their body, how much the sequencing of amino acids in their chromosomes is also a part of their story, and how much is stereotyped perception by the observer (Frey 1999). For an empirical study in this field see Koemeda-Lutz & Peter (2002). We, however, will limit our discussion to the relevance of Reich's insight for the empathic therapist. But first, let me just tell you some short stories.

The three Bioenergetic teachers with whom I first bonded and who therefore had a deep impact on me were Al Lowen, John Pierrakos, and Bill Walling. They were the giants on whose shoulders I stand today. They were the original three founders of the Bioenergetic Institute. Being male myself and having been taught and in therapy with all three of these men, there is a massive lack of female perspective in what I bring to you today. Thank God that Helen will have the last word tomorrow! Since Bill Walling was my first and main therapist and since he died while we were still working together, I probably do not, even after all these years, have a clear view of him. So let me share a bit of my experience of Al and John. Like many of us from that era, I felt that they complemented each other in a deeply beautiful way. Al was the brilliant, explicit man who could see so clearly and deeply the person before him. He never said and I never sensed that he focused much on his own most personal feelings in grasping the essence of his patient. Rather, as he once told me in a session when I was the patient, he listened to my words, but what he really was tuned to was the moment when, out of awareness, my deeper, nonverbal self would reveal itself to him in a fleeting gesture of my eyes, my torso, and so on. John, on the other hand, was the deeply intuitive man who literally closed his eyes when he wanted to know what was going on within you. As I sat with him, I often had the impression that he was finding me somewhere deep inside of himself. All of you know that Al Lowen's name is synonymous with Bioenergetics, but those of you who are younger may not know that both John and Al had an enormous impact on Bioenergetics in their twenty plus years of passionate work together. My story underlines two points for us today: (1) Bioenergetics does give us tools to see and feel the psychosomatic truth of a person, and Al and John were both master clinicians. But ultimately, we ourselves are the unique instruments which attune to the other's psyche-soma. (2) My second point is that (at least in my own experience of them) Al and John, in their preferred way of understanding me, tended not to be responding to aspects of me of which I was aware, and in this sense, were not being empathic.

IV. What are the limits to how much we can consiously (explicitly) see of a person's story as opposed to (implicitly) sensing its depths and nuances

Let me start with a vignette about learning to trust your own intuition, which is a necessary but perhaps not sufficient condition for being empathic. Many years ago when the Bioenergetic Institute was young, there was a big workshop in New York where Bill, John and Al each worked in a different corner of this huge room – I cannot remember who worked in the fourth corner. Participants would move around the room and be worked with by each of my three idealized attachment figures. It was both frightening and deeply relieving to discover that Bill, John and Al each focused and worked on completely different issues with the same person. The message landed: Either there was not a story that could be read in the form and motility of each workshop participant's body, or *that story was so complex*, that each of my three mentors trusted themselves to work with that part of the story that spoke to them at the moment.

Regarding how much anyone can know of another person's story, I hope you will not fear that I have taken leave of my senses if I ask you (show poster) why Mona Lisa is smiling. This is, of course, a question that has been pondered for almost five hundred years, so forgive yourselves if you do not have the answer.

Although I have no expertise in the field of fine arts and am therefore not at all qualified to say what makes *Mona Lisa* the masterpiece it is, I believe Leonardo da Vinci has something to teach us about empathy, about how much we can fathom the experience of another. Leonardo is said to have been both a consummate master of the details of nature and a man fascinated by the enigmatic in life. In *Mona Lisa*, according to E.H. Gombrich in *The Story of Art* (www.artchive.com/artchive/L/leonardo/monalisa_text.jpg.html) Leonardo employed a technique which he himself had invented called »sfumato«. In »sfumato« the blurred outline and mellowed colors allow one form to merge with another and always leave something to our imagination. Gombrich, the art critic, describes how Leonardo has deliberately left two crucial features of Mona Lisa's facial expression indistinct: the corners of her eyes and the corners of her mouth. This, says Gombrich (and many other experts), is at least part of why Lisa looks so amazingly alive: »She really seems to look at us and to have a mind of her own. Like a living being, she seems to change before our eyes and to look a little different every time we come back to her« (p. 1). So Leonardo has created a work of art which both challenges and illuminates the clinical art and science of empathy. With these two crucial areas of facial anatomy indistinct, we are never quite sure in what mood *Mona Lisa* is really looking at us. Her expression always seems just to elude us. And naturally, each time we stand in front of her we receive an expression that is colored by the state and mood we are in at the moment.

Of course, as Bioenergetic therapists we work with the expression of the entire body, not just the face. However when we look to most recent state of the art clinical research on implicit, empathic communication, they involve head orientation, visual gaze, vocal behaviors and facial expression. Ekman et al. (1980), for instance, created a system for coding all possible emotional expressions of the facial muscles. Once you have explicitly learned this system, they claim that you will be able to read what is on the heart and mind in the fleeting nuances of facial expression ... an ability which comes naturally only to the occasional person with a special intuitive talent. So, in a way, the five hundred people in the world who have been certified in the facial action coding system could be called »Bioenergetic specialists of the face«. This system has been around for over twenty years, and is quoted extensively in the literature. But why have more therapists *not* flocked to a system which claims to enable us to read minds? Some therapists are just too lazy to learn another system, but others probably agree with Irwin Yalom's (1989) conclusion in an essay entitled *Two Smiles*. Yalom speaks to the dilemma at the heart of being an empathic therapist. While we desire to know another deeply, whether it be our child, our lover or our patient, they remain ultimately unknowable. Yalom's patient smiles twice; each time the smile expresses such a nuanced, complex reality within her that no one could possibly grasp its meaning without knowing many interlocking details of her current and past life. Even Ekman et al. would not have known what Yalom's patient was smiling about. Yalom makes the further point that a patient is diminished if we assume that we can fully know them. I agree with him. In fact, if neuroscience ever advances to the point where it can take pictures of the secret recesses of our minds, we may have to throw away the pictures.

So too with the workshop participants in whom Al Lowen, John Pierrakos and Bill Walling each saw something different. Perhaps even more than the Mona Lisa, being alive, they changed from moment to moment, and as they met the gaze or did not meet the unique gaze of Bill, John or Al, in split second time, a nonverbal limbic conversation suggested the material for the next »session«.

Finally back to *Mona Lisa*. By now most of you have probably figured out why she is smiling. She is smiling because A) she thinks it is funny that people are trying to figure out why she is smiling B) she is grateful that Leonardo with his genius and his »sfumato« has given her such richness and complexity. Lisa is not unlike the real people who come to our therapy rooms. The more we realize our conscious, explicit grasp of them is just the tip of the iceberg (or better yet – dialectic diagram with explicit/implicit systems), the less their implicit mysteries will elude our grasp.

V. What is the quality of or capacity for presence which allows us to understand the experience of another?

The answer is that we do not exactly know, although we know a lot and what we know is coming closer to a somatopsychic unity. We can demonstrate, for instance, that the quality of attunement between a mother and child becomes the balance or imbalance in the parasympathetic and sympathetic branches of the child's autonomic nervous system. The child's attachment experience, as Allan Schore proposes, has been hard-wired into his right limbic system as a model of relationships to come. We can describe the empathic process on many levels of organization, and they are all valid. There is *empathy as »limbic resonance«* (Lewis et al. 2000a, p.63), empathy as a »conversation between limbic systems« (Buck 1994, p. 266), empathy as feeling the patient's physical sensations in your own body (Havens 1979), empathy as becoming that part of you which is closest to the patient (Kramer 1989). As we get down to the neuroanatomical level, let me digress briefly to note that Allan Schore (2003) has creatively integrated an impressive body of neurobiological research on the empathic process which points to the right limbic and orbitofrontal cortical areas of the brain. It is his specific hypothesis that empathy involves a right-brain to right-brain conversation. The right orbitofrontal cortex, anterior cingulate (?) and amygdala for instance, are critically and directly involved in evaluating facial expressions, direction of eye gaze and other nonverbal s that reveal what is going on in another person. This information, plus the autonomic state of one's own body is integrated by the orbitofrontal cortex with other cortical areas. To understand much of the original neuroscience research from which Schore builds his hypotheses requires a technical background which I do not have. Schore helps us by borrowing from the field of physics:

»In physics, a property of resonance is harmonic sympathetic vibration, which is the tendency of one resonance system to enlarge and amplify through matching the resonance frequency pattern of another resonance system« (p. 79).

Happily, Schore tells us on the same page, tells us in clinical terms how to do »harmonic sympathetic vibration«:

»The attuned, intuitive therapist, from the first point of contact, is learning the moment-to-moment rhythmic structures of the patient and is relatively flexibly and fluidly modifying his/her own behavior to fit that structure« (p. 79).

Let me give you an example of how I, Bob Lewis, do this, or rather how this happens to me:

My patient, for instance will bring up material about how depraved he feels, or how cosmically alone he feels or how wildly grandiose – the common factor being that the quality or attribute he presents is not one with which I can readily identify. It is beyond the confines of the image of Bob Lewis that I ordinarily entertain. So my initial inner reaction is something like, »wow, what an awful problem *that* person has!« Then, as moments or minutes go by, I slowly get in touch with aspects of myself that indeed are resonant with my patient's issue. For instance, Paul, a very sad lonely patient of mine in his early forties was lamenting with self-loathing that, not only had he never had sex other than with a prostitute, but that he had never had whatever it took to suggest the same to any woman. As you might suspect, I was initially comfortably ensconced in an image of myself as nothing like this unfortunate man. At first what came to mind were youthful adventures that attested to my virility. But then, as I sat resonating with my unhappy patient, I slowly remembered that I knew exactly what he was talking about. When I was about fourteen years old, just beginning high school, I was afraid to kiss my first girlfriend, I shall call her Susan, at the end of our dates ... even though her younger brother, at Susan's asking, had told me in the locker room at school that his sister Susan really liked me a lot. So, as I surrender my defenses and ideal images to my patient's material, I am more in touch with my vulnerabilities, which enhances my capacity to be empathic. I did not tell Paul about the painful recollection of Susan which had brought me closer to him. I would have been far too ashamed. But perhaps something silent did come back to him from my facial expression and a change in the timbre of my voice.

Beebe and Lachmann (2002) have done extensive mother-infant research on facial mirroring. They relate the following data to early experiences of empathy:

> »How each partner's face attracts and responds to the other's is one of the foundations of intimacy throughout life ... to the degree that facial mirroring interactions are positively correlated, so that the partners are changing in the same affective direction, the infant represents the expectation of matching and being matched ... (the concomitant arousal pattern and mode of self-regulation are part of the representation), the infant represents the experience of seeing the mother's face continuously changing to become more similar to his or her own; the infant also represents the experience of his or her own face constantly changing to become more similar to the mother's face. These »matching« experiences contribute to feeling known, attuned to and on the same wave length. Each partner affects the other so as to match affective direction, and this matching provides each with a behavioral basis for entering into the others feeling state« (p. 98).

What is some of the extensive evidence that, as we all intuitively know, »timing is everything«, not only in infancy, but across the life-span? Actually, it was adult studies that first suggested that timing and rhythm alone, irrespective of the content of behavior, were powerful organizers of communication. Vital messages are sent between partners in this temporal code. Beebe and Lachman (2002) report, for instance, that when:

> »Asked to converse about a neutral topic, unacquainted adults were found to match the purely temporal rhythms of dialogue, irrespective of the content of the speech ... Of special relevance was the finding of a relationship between matching rhythms of dialogue, and empathy and affect. When the adult strangers matched rhythms, they liked each other more and perceived each other as warmer and more similar than they did when their rhythms did not match. Thus similarity in the temporal pattern of communicative behavior is associated with interpersonal attraction and empathy.
>
> Conversely, a speaker who speaks very rapidly and barely pauses long enough for the partner to get a word in edgewise powerfully interferes with the exchange: The partner may become frustrated and »tune out«. Subtle changes in timing, such as hesitation or interruption, also affect the listener's experience of the relatedness. In adult conversation we depend on the matching of temporal patterns to know that the other is »tuned in« and to take turns smoothly« (p. 99).

In addition to the crucial importance of head orientation and direction of gaze, Beebe and Lachmann cite Trout and Rosenfeld (1980) as finding that during psychotherapy sessions (therapist and patient sitting, facing each other), a report of higher rapport by patient and therapist is associated with a higher incidence of leaning the upper bodies toward each other and holding the limbs in mirror image postures. One may infer from this that rapport is disturbed if either partner displays any degree of orientational aversion.

How better to close this section than with a vignette from Donald Winnicott, an early and past master of implicit empathy. Here he is in procedural mode:

> »The detail I have chosen for description has to do with the absolute need this patient had, from time to time, to be in contact with me.
>
> A variety of intimacies were tried out, chiefly those that belong to infant feeding and management. There were violent episodes. Eventually it came about that she and I were together with her head in my hands. Without deliberate action on the part of each of us there developed a rocking rhythm. The rhythm was rather a rapid one, about seventy per minute (c.f. heart beat), and I had to do some work to adapt to this rate. Nevertheless, there we were with mutuality expressed in terms of slight but persistent rocking movement. We were communicating with each other without words« (p. 258).

VI. To what extent can the implicit and procedural become explicit?

Jeremy Holmes (1993), the author of a wonderful biography of Bowlby which illuminates attachment theory, starts us off on a somewhat fatalistic note, depending on whether you are a good therapist or a bad one. Good therapists, he says, »find themselves automatically mirroring their patient's levels of speech volume and their posture« (p. 156). Peter Fernald (2000), a Bioenergetic colleague, says the following about his attempts to respond empathically:

> »I try to position myself, my body, physically or imaginatively in a manner that closely resembles my client's bodily state – his or her depth and rate of breathing, clenched fist, frozen pelvis, and so forth. I try my best to embody my client's experience, to walk in his or her psychological, emotional, body-armored footprints.« (p. 3–4).

Peter is describing what most of us try to do, each in our own way. Helen Resneck-Sannes (2002) in her recent article, attunes to and resonates with her client's body. The Southern California Training Program encourages its students, from the first moments, that they look at and listen to their dyadic partner, to assume the bodily attitude of the person and feel his or her story in their own bodies. I myself have learned to trust and value the empathic implicit knowing in my hands. They often know how to be with my patient before I do. I have also learned to watch the hands of my patient, as they often tell me, in the moment, what I cannot otherwise see and what my patient cannot tell me. We must not forget, however, that to confront our patient with implicit information that is beyond what they are willing or able to tolerate, is to be unempathic (but this is another vignette).

Turning to some empirical data, Beebe et al. (1997) working on »Mechanisms of Facial Mirroring and Precursors of Empathy« find that:

> »Similarity of behavior implies a congruence of feeling, a relationship between matching and empathy. How might this work? Two areas of study suggest potential mechanisms for the precursors of empathy and ways of translating matching behavior into the sharing of subjective states. The work of Ekman (1983) and Zajonc (1985) shows that matching the expression of the other is highly correlated with matching the physiological arousal pattern. Ekman showed that a particular facial expression is associated with a particular pattern of autonomic activity. *Reproducing the expression of another person produces a similar physiological state in the onlooker.* This mechanism of empathy is facial matching, which is *correlated with physiological matching. This mechanism of empathy may be equally relevant to adult face-to-face therapy interactions*« (p. 161).

Beebe (2003) is both humble and optimistic about how much implicit process can be consciously focused to improve the empathic quality of our clinical work. Beebe tells us that she happened to see herself in a videotaped session with a traumatized patient, Dolores. She, Beebe, discovered that she does a great deal of what Freedman et al. (1978) call self-regulatory touching. Beebe explains:

> »I did know that at times I rub my hands together, particularly when they hurt a little, but I did not realize how much I do it ... it is very unlikely that I would ever have become aware of this behavior without the aid of the videotape. Such behaviors may remain out of awareness of both patient and analyst but nevertheless are perceived at a subliminal level and operate as information to both ... During an episode in the treatment of Dolores, when I felt her to be inaccessible I began to rub my feet together. I recognized it as a gesture that I had used throughout my childhood to put myself to sleep at night. I commented to Dolores that I noticed that I had been rubbing my feet together. Dolores was then able to come forward and make the observation that it happened just when she was refusing a comforting interpretation that I was giving her, so I comforted myself. I very much appreciated her observation. A very intimate moment followed in which we both felt closer, and she expressed regret at having been so inaccessible« (p. 133).

I find that Beebe's nonverbal behavior was brought into Doroles' focal awareness by Beebe's explicit comment. This willingness to explicitly share what is usually private information seems to have touched an empathic cord in Dolores – empathic to the discomfort that she was causing Beebe. Dolores then delivered back to Beebe an implicitly sensed, explicitly phrased, empathic gift. Beebe (2003, in press) goes on to cite Karlen Lyons-Ruth, another exciting mother-infant researcher, and member of the Boston Process of Change Study Group. Lyons-Ruth (1998), coined the term »implicit relational knowing« to better describe what goes on in the empathic process. Beebe tells us that:

> »Because implicit relational knowing is predominantly outside of awareness, and rarely in focal attention, Lyons-Ruth argues that much of the subtlety and complexity of what the analyst knows is never put into words. It is for this reason that my examination of the videotaped interactions revealed much about my behavior that I could not have described without them, and why it was difficult to find a language to describe them« (p. 58).

Beebe's patient, Dolores, told her that she had also gotten something valuable from viewing the videos:

> »In watching the video Dolores discovered that I was seeing what she herself ›carried‹ in her face and body, or ›sensed‹ about herself, without being able to describe it verbally. Seeing my face seeing her, and hearing my sounds responding to hers, alerted her to her own inner affective reality ... Dolores would find herself ›putting on‹ my facial expressions while watching the video. By ›wearing‹ my face Dolores became more affectively aware of her own inner experience, presumably through the proprioceptive feedback of her face, ... as well as the feedback from various physiological arousal systems« (p. 49).

So, finally, it is not easy for Beebe to say what she has explicitly learned. The video helped by confronting her with how little she was aware of what she was doing when she was with her patient. Beebe also says that »much of my nonverbal behavior with her (Dolores) was based on what the infants had taught me« (p.58). Beebe concludes, »We can teach ourselves to observe these implicit, nonverbal interactions simultaneously in ourselves and in our patients, expanding our own awareness and where useful, that of the patient.« (p.58). Not being a professor, I can say this more simply. Our implicit and explicit selves become more user-friendly with each other. Some of you, perhaps many of you at this conference, already do this. Actually it is not so much about **doing** anything as it is about learning to be with ourselves and patients in a different way. We cannot directly look into the face of God, or even into the sun. But we are excited and we become more resonant when an explicit glimpse:

»reveals our lives lit by the diffuse glow of a second sun we never see.« (Lewis et al. 2000b, p. 111).

VII. What are the implications for bioenergetics of recent research that puts implicit, relational, nonverbal process at the heart of our therapy endeavor

A) *A time to feel proud*: Most of us body-oriented therapists feel confirmed and validated by empirical research that stresses the enormous importance throughout the life-span of the non-verbal, sensory-motor encoding of experience. Everyone seems to be discovering that experience from the first few years of life or at any age, if the experience has been traumatic, can best be accessed implicitly, on a body level. The meaning is in the rhythm, the music beneath the words. Many of us have suffered considerable shame that we do allegedly aggressive, sexual, generally noisy therapy. Our work has generally not been accepted as serious, legitimate, mainstream. Perhaps it is quite different in Brasil, but in Europe and North America a therapy that values the body as highly as the mind or the spirit is out of line with the larger culture.

So, I agree that it is more than time to be proud of our heritage. I agree with Helen Resneck-Sannes (2002) in her recent article that we have been trained to be aware of the tension and form and flow and sound and warmth of the body; its sensory-motor language should be more in our awareness than that of our non-body-oriented colleagues.

Indeed Helen's clinical vignettes in the same article set a high standard for anyone. The nuanced manner in which she attunes to her patient's tolerance for arousal, nearness, preferred mode of communication, and to her own bodily cues, are of a high caliber. There is similar case material in the excellent, above cited book by Beebe and Lachmann (2002). They also focus their awareness on the intensity and duration and rhythm of gaze behaviors and speech pattern and posture and orientation. They seem much more limited, however than Helen and most somatically oriented psychotherapists, in that most of what goes on below the neck is still taboo.

B) *But not too proud*: Although I could stop here, let me get myself into some trouble, by challenging us not to congratulate ourselves too quickly. Regarding the validity or legitimacy of our work as perceived by the larger community, I have three quick points: (l) First, let those of us who have the ability, strive, as Christa Ventling (2002) urges us to in her journal article, to bring more empirical research to our work. (2) Second, let us be careful how we use words like »energy« which we define in a way that contradicts the laws of physics and third, it is my own feeling that we should all, myself included, read the literature and cite it when we use others' material.

Back to empathy's biggest issue ... if I really grasp that the conscious, explicit process is the tip of the implicit iceberg (earth's core is perhaps a warmer metaphor than iceberg … and that core to core messages travel in fractions of a second … *then I never know anything clearly for more than a moment or two* … I have no choice but to »live in the question« (Michael Maley 1995). There is a deep paradox for us here. We need to question what we do and strive to empirically validate its efficacy. It is wise to expect our Bioenergetic students to have a reasonable explanation for their interventions, an explanation which they can state explicitly. At the same time, the students must learn that their perceptions and behavior are being influenced by an almost instantaneous process moving, largely out of awareness, between them and their patients. This is a humbling process for me after thirty-five years of practice. It cannot be that easy for a beginning student who wants answers to quell his anxieties. Helen Resneck-Sannes (2002) once again strikes a note of optimism here: »Because somatic therapists are trained to be aware of their internal body processes, what is unconscious for the analyst, exists to a greater degree in the conscious awareness of the Bioenergetically trained Analyst.« (p. 115).

I am less certain than Helen about this for a number of reasons:

I) First, Helen was barely born when I began my Bioenergetic career, and I am a prisoner of my generation's perspective. For many years Bioenergetic Analysis was taught as a one-person psychology. Show me, for instance, a place in one of Alexander's books where his awareness of his own internal body process helps him to sense the depth or specificity of his patient's body problem. Of course what we have experienced and been taught in our Bioenergetic careers varies from place to place, and we each approach our craft with our own models and innate preferences. It is true that a second and third generation of Bioenergetic therapists and teachers have brought more of a two-person psychology into our work (Schindler 2002). But it is also true that, as we speak, our Institute is struggling to integrate this newer relational perspective without losing the power of our psychosomatic approach.

II) Second, just a few years ago, when I was one of the faculty, during the final, »supervisory« part of a Bioenergetic training program where the advanced students did »sessions« in front of the group, I found that, under the pressure of being observed and judged, it was the rare student that felt safe enough to tune into what he was feeling and sensing about himself, his »client« and the interaction. Instead, he went up into his head and tried to figure out what to do, and predictably, what he »did« was not well-attuned/empathic for his client. The big news here is not that the students could not stay with the moment-by-moment process between them and their »clients«. The big news is that most of us, even after thirty years do the same thing as the students whenever we are threatened by what our patients bring to the therapy. The kind of primitive, chaotic, visceral (gut-wrenching) material that has no words and is delivered into the room sensory-motorically, tends to be threatening to most of us. It is to me.

III) Thirdly, the problem is even more basic than this. We are the problem. Have you forgotten that, as Bob Hilton (1988–89) once said, »we have all been broken« (p.74)? Have you forgotten that, as Michael Maley (1995) reminds us, we are wounded healers? I find that whenever I become engaged in trying to be a good therapist and to capture the alive interaction in my mind, I tend to miss being in the moment with my patient. I did this often years ago, long before I described the syndrome of cephalic shock. But my implicit knowing, even then, tried to help me with the shock in my head, the shock which was keeping me from a more full-bodied attunement with my patients. Moments after the patient would leave my office, both in the same instant, my hand would slap my forehead like this (gesture) and I would realize that I had missed the obvious while I was thinking.

Of course, we do also have to think and talk to our patients. At times we have to stop the split-second action and figure out what has been enacted between us and the patient. But I speak of the basic wound in us which limits our empathic contact with our patients. With many variations, this wound is about our not being a good enough, valuable human being. Thus, often without realizing it, we try to redeem that broken self by being a good therapist. We can try to become a therapist who is most implicitly attuned to subtle sensory-motor cues in ourselves and our patients. But if we also remember that we have been broken, and are still deeply wounded, we will find, as Bob Hilton (2000) put it so beautifully, »... that piece of me that had been hiding behind my therapeutic mode of interaction, namely the value of my real self to another person« (p. 10).

So I earlier presented the vignette where I felt safe enough with my unlovable self to allow it to come into the room with Paul, my similarly inadequate patient. In fact, I usually come out looking like a pretty good therapist in my vignettes. But wouldn't it be refreshing if I got real and presented a string of empathic failures, or at least some disruptions and repairs. The latest research shows that even mothers and children who will later test as securely attached, spend only about one third of their time in matched states. However, within two seconds, 70% of the unmatched states returned to a match, and both the mothers and infants both influenced the repair! The child's implicit neurobiology is organizing the expectation that it can participate in repairing affectively painful disruptions (Tronick and Cohn 1989). Something like this also happens in an adult therapy situation when things work out.

In this next vignette things did not work out. The patient presents with oral symptoms, collapsed bony chest, shallow breathing. You suggest breathing deeply to give him more charge in his upper body. He tells you that he hates the suggestion, that whenever he has tried it in the past, he feels light-headed, but nothing happens ... it feels mechanical and manipulative to him. He elaborates further: »My breathing«, he says, »has to come from something that I am doing, something that feels alive and genuine. I will breathe when I feel fucking ready to breathe!« Being an empathic therapist, you stop your suggestions and ask what might feel »alive and genuine« to the patient. He seems quite stunned, then increasingly touched that you are interested enough in him to drop your breathing agenda for the moment. Then, as he lies back across the stool and some minutes go by in silence, you sense a deadness in his stillness ... his breathing is barely discernable ... you sense the deadness in your own chest, and, although you are quite frightened ... you are not comfortable with death ... you tolerate the still, empty sensation and your fear, and you notice that your breathing has become very slow and shallow ... slowly, to your amazement, your dread begins to lessen and you even sense a kind of peacefulness come over you ... after several more minutes, your patient turns to you and can barely find the words to thank you for allowing him, he says, to luxuriate in his apnea (not breathing).

As it happens, I can tell you the patient's name: Bob Lewis. The name is real, but the session is a fiction. It's the session Bob never had. As he lay across the Bioenergetic stool, Bob never had the courage nor the words to tell his Bioenergetic therapist how ashamed he was of the deadness in his chest ... to tell him that he hated him for not realizing what he needed but could not tell him: that his inner flame was very low. That he, Bob, would not or could not breathe from the dead place in his chest unless his therapist could be with him in the Valley of the Shadow of Death. The words he never found were: »Approach me in a soulful way ... my spirit will quicken if you nourish its flame ... and I will breathe from within.«

In my closing vignette, I am the therapist, and I appear to have learned, after many empathic disruptions which were *not* repaired, how to be with my patient Florence in a way that *would* have been helpful to Bob Lewis and his Bioenergetic stool. Florence was not easy for me. Typically, we would seem to be conversing in left hemispheric, explicit, adult language, but I would become confused, annoyed and anxious as the room filled with primal, visceral, intense rage, pain and futility. My typical attempt to defend myself was to try to regain my equilibrium via a quick retreat to my left hemisphere from which I would point out in a voice both plaintive and irritated something inconsistent, something that did not make sense to me about Florence's words and feelings. Florence would be stunned by my empathic abandonment and things would escalate beyond repair.

However, Florence and I both suffer from unrelenting hope, so we are still working together. We recently had a session that suggested that there may be a realistic basis for the hope. Florence was in the midst of a deep experience of mourning that neither I nor her father had been able to give her more of what she needed. Perhaps most importantly, she needs to be able to scream the enormous feelings of rage and disappointment and let her body twist in »agony«, as she puts it afterwards, without having to worry about me. So I need to be able to feel my face become twisted and to tolerate the heat and heaviness in my head and chest. As Florence's »agonized« feelings about having been failed by both me and her father fill the room, I can feel emptiness, sadness and pain in my own (rather oral) rebuilt chest, essentially the same Bob Lewis chest that lay over the Bioenergetic stool thirty-five years ago. Once or twice Florence says, »I wasn't touched«. As I hear a particularly raw cry from Florence and notice a slight resonant tender sound come out of me, I tell her that I do not know if physically touching her would be for my need or for hers. I am not sure whether my touch would interfere with the fullness of her experiencing having been failed. Florence tells me how precious it is to her that I share my not knowing. After a few minutes, I decide to put my hand on her left shoulder, near her heart. After a while Florence moves my hand away, indicating that it is not helpful. As she resumes the painful grieving, I notice my hands are clasped together in a gesture that both surprises and comforts me. The gesture feels very strong. My hands, clasped together in an act of solidarity, seem to be bringing me comfort and a sense of unity. They tell me how fragmenting it feels to stay with Florence's helplessness to be helped and my helplessness to help. They reassure me that I am whole and worthwhile even as a failed healer.

The session with Florence that I just shared, demonstrates the implicit use of my hands to better regulate myself (I felt attuned to by my hands) so that I can maintain better empathic contact with my patient. But I did not intentionally clasp my hands together. That may be the best I can do in explaining empathy: Somehow, in immersing myself in this shadowy subject, my focal awareness has expanded to include more of my implicit behavior. My empathic resonance becomes deeper and wiser when I surrender to the shame of not knowing and not seeing clearly. Only then can I, and all of us, sense »the diffuse glow of a sun we never see«. (Lewis et al. 2000b, p. 111).

References

Beebe, B., Lachmann, F. & Jaffe, J. (1997): Mother-infant interaction structures and presymbolic self and object representations. Psychoanalytic Dialogues 7(2) 133–182.

Beebe, B. & Lachmann, F. (2002): Infant research and adult treatment. Hillsdale, NJ (The Analytic Press, Inc.).

Beebe, B. (2003, in press): Faces-in relation: Forms of intersubjectivity in an adult treatment of early trauma. Psychoanalytic Dialogues.

Buck, R. (1994): The neuropsychology of communication: Spontaneous and symbolic aspects. Journal of Pragmatics, 22, 265–278.

Ekman,P. (1983): Autonomic nervous system activity distinguishes among emotions. Science, 221, 1208–1210.

Ekman, P. Friesen, W., & Ancoli, S. (1980): Facial signs of emotional experience. Journal of Personality and Social Psychology, 39, 1125–1134.

Fernald, P. (2000): Bioenergetics and modes of therapeutic action: A response to Martha Stark and Robert Hilton. Presented at the International Conference on Bioenergetic Analysis. Montebello, Canada, May, 2000.

Fogel, A. (1993): Developing through relationships. Chicago (University of Chicago Press).

Freedman, N. Barroso, F., Bucci, W. & Grand, S. (1978): The bodily manifestations of listening. Psychoanalysis and Contemporary Thought, 1, 156–194.

Frey, S. (1999): Die Macht des Bildes. Der Einfluss der nonverbalen Kommunikation auf Kultur und Politik. Bern (Hans Huber).

Gombrich, E., www.artchive.com/artchive/L/leonardo/monalisa_text.jpg.html

Havens, L. (1979): Explorations in the uses of language in psychotherapy: Complex empathic statements. Psychiatry, 42, 40–48.

Hilton, R. (1988/89): Narcissism and the therapist's resistance to working with the body. Bioenergetic Analysis. The Clinical Journal of the International Institute for Bioenergetic Analysis 3(2) 45–74.

Hilton, R. (2000): Bioenergetics and modes of therapeutic action. Presented at the International Conference on Bioenergetic Analysis. Montebello, Canada, May, 2000.

Holmes, J. (1993): Attachment theory and the practice of psychotherapy. John Bowlby and attachment theory (149–176). London (Routledge).

Jaffe, J., Beebe, B., Feldstein, S., Crown, C. & Jasnow, M. (2001): Rhythms of dialogue in early infancy. Monographs of the Society for Research in Child Development, 66(2) serial No. 264, 1–132.

Kramer, P. (1989): Is empathy necessary? Pp. 129–153 in: Moments of engagement. New York (Penguin Books USA, Inc.).

Koemeda-Lutz, M. & Peter, H. (2002): What do human bodies tell us? – In search of statistically significant empirical confirmation for the »language of the body«. A study in Bioenergetic body diagnostics. Bioenergetic Analysis. The Clinical Journal of the International Institute for Bioenergetic Analysis Vol.13 (1): 77–94 (published in German (2001): Psychotherapie Forum 9 (2) 51–61).

Lewis, Th., Amini, F., Lannon, R. (2000a): Archimedes' principle. Pp. 35–65 in: A general theory of love. New York (Vintage).

Lewis, Th., Amini, F., Lannon, R. (2000b): Gravity's incarnation. Pp. 100–120 in: A general theory of love. New York (Vintage).

Lyons-Ruth, K. (1998): Implicit relational knowing. Infant Mental Health Journal, 19, 282–291.

Maley, M. (1995): Living in the question. Minneapolis (Bodysmart Publications).

Reich, W. (1933, in German: 1949): Character Analysis. New York (Noonday Press:Farrar, Straus & Cudahy).

Resneck-Sannes, H. (2002): Psychobiology of affects: Implications for a somatic psychotherapy. Bioenergetic Analysis. The Clinical Journal of the International Institute for Bioenergetic Analysis 13(1) 111–122.

Sander, L. (1977): The regulation of exchange in the infant-caretaker system and some aspects of the context-content relationship. In M. Lewis & L. Rosenblum (Eds.): Interaction, conversation, and the development of language (pp. 133–156). New York (Wiley).

Schindler, P. (2002): Geschichte und Entwicklung der Bioenergetischen Analyse. Pp.27–48 in: Koemeda-Lutz, M. (Ed.): Körperpsychotherapie – Bioenergetische Konzepte im Wandel. Basel (Schwabe Verlag).

Schore, A. (2003): Affect regulation and the repair of the self. New York (W. W. Norton & Co., Inc.).

Stark, M. (1999): Modes of therapeutic action. Northvale, NJ (Jason Aronson, Inc.).

Stern, D. (1985): The interpersonal world of the infant. New York (Basic Books, Inc.).

Tansey, M. & Burke, W. (1989): Understanding countertransference: From projective identification to empathy. Hillsdale, NJ (Analytic Press).

Tronick, E. (1989): Emotions and emotional communication in infants. The American Psychologist, 44, 112–119.

Tronick, E., & Cohn, J. (1989): Infant mother face-to-face interaction: Age and gender differences in coordination and miscoordination. Child Development, 59, 85–92.

Trout, D. & Rosenfeld, H. (1980): The effect of postural lean and body congruence on the judgement of psychotherapeutic rapport. Journal of Nonverbal Behavior, 4, 176–190.

Ventling, C. (2002): The significance of scientific research for Bioenergetics. Bioenergetic Analysis. The Clinical Journal of the International Institute for Bioenergetic Analysis 13(1) 1–20.

Webster's New World College Dictionary, Fourth Edition (2001). Foster City, CA (IDG Books Worldwide, Inc.).

Weiss (cited on page 1)

Winnicott, D. (1989): Mother-infant experience of mutuality. Pp. 251–260 in: Psychoanalytic explorations. Cambridge, MA (Harvard Univ. Press).

Yalom, I. (1989): Two Smiles. Pp. 167–186 in: Love's Executioner. New York (Harper Collins).
Zajonc, R. (1985): Emotion and facial efference: a theory reclaimed. Science, 228, 15–22.

Robert Lewis, M.D.,
155 East 91st Street #1B,
New York NY 10128, USA,
e-mail: boblewis@inch.com

Bioenergetics: Past, Present and Future

Helen Resneck-Sannes

Several people helped me with this speech and I want to acknowledge them. Thank you to Michael and Sylvia Conant and to Virginia and Bob Hilton for helping me to organize the speech as well as clarify certain concepts. I also want to thank my husband, David and daughter, Myrrhia for their love, support and intelligence and a special thank you to Myrrhia for her writing skills. It is with deep appreciation I thank my primary Bioenergetic trainers, David Finlay and Eleanor Greenlee. Without their commitment to their own process as well as to Bioenergetics and the Institute, I would not be here. Finally, I want to thank Jim Miller. From my first time at Whistler, he encouraged me to become a trainer and a teacher. I still miss him a great deal.

And then ... the people of Brazil. What can I say? At conferences over the years I would hear the Brazilians dancing and singing until late in the evening. At first I was resentful, and then I realized that I was jealous. I wanted to be having that much fun. Every year when asked where we should have the next conference, I would write, Brazil. I have been waiting for this conference for years and it is a real pleasure to be here.

The literature I discuss has all been written in English because that is the only language I feel adequate to read with real understanding. I will also cover some of the same material as Bob Lewis. I admire his ability to so beautifully describe empathic attunement as it is experienced in the soma/psyche of the therapist.

> Morris asks his son, now aged 10, if he knows about the birds and the bees. »I don't want to know«, the child said, bursting into tears.
>
> Confused, the father asked his son what was wrong.
>
> »Oh Dad«, he sobbed, »at age six I got the ›there's no Santa‹ speech. At age seven I got the ›there's no Easter bunny‹ speech. If you're going to tell me now that grown-ups really have sex, I've got nothing left to live for!«

I thought I would have your attention if I mentioned the word sex; and to put you at ease, I'm not going to announce that the future of Bioenergetics shouldn't still have sex as an important aspect of the therapy. In 12 step programs for addictions, people stand up and tell their truth. They say things like: »My name is ... and I'm an alcoholic, sex addict, cocaine abuser ...«, whatever. Well, I'm going to stand up here in front of you all today and tell the truth. »My name is Helen Resneck-Sannes and I entered Bioenergetic Analysis to have ›The Big O‹«. You know, the full bodied orgasm from head to toe, from the inside out; that orgasm described in the book, *For Whom The Bell Tolls*, that causes the earth to move off its axis.

When I began my Bioenergetic therapy, I was having good sex with my husband, regular orgasms, but Lowen and Reich were describing something quite powerful. At the time I was confused about how this incredible orgasm occurred without a partner; and only later came to understand that the orgasmic reflex was an energy wave that circulated throughout the body, creating a harmonious rhythm that was quite separate from sexual intercourse. Well, I think I've had ›The Big O‹ a couple of times; if not ›The Big O‹, I definitely experienced streamings that coursed through my entire body producing a harmonic vibratory sensation. However, in 1984 or 1985 during a talk in Berkeley, California, Lowen admitted that he was 74 years old and had never had ›The Big O‹ and doubted that he ever would, as he was getting older. Although he wished for a complete orgasm reflex, he had become aware that harmonic streamings on the mat does not necessarily indicate a healthy person or even a healthy sexual relationship.

Although I'm beginning the talk with a personal story, I think my involvement with Bioenergetics mirrors the development of it as a theory and practice. The reality is that Bioenergetics is a therapy being created in our offices, in our training programs, in our writings, and at these conferences. And we have a new curriculum thanks to the commitment, tenacity, and good will of our faculty and especially to the writers Guy Tonella and Violaine De Clerck.

As I see it, three major paradigms emerged over time and influenced the members of the Bioenergetic community and their practice of therapy. The first paradigm in Bioenergetics as developed by John Pierrakkos and Alexander Lowen viewed the person from the outside. Open the armor and the person would be free. When I began therapy, I had some concept of what a Bioenergetic Analysis might look like. It quickly changed. During the first few sessions, my therapist read my body and taught me how to ground. After that, every session began with me in a squatting position up against the wall. We both hoped that my legs would tire, that I would give in and allow softer feelings to emerge. By giving up control, supposedly, the armor around my chest would open; and subsequently, my heart. I didn't realize at the time the profound effect such an experience would have on me. As my friends saw me become more open with my emotions and willing to expose my vulnerability, they also enrolled in Bioenergetic therapy.

As the practice of Bioenergetics developed, a second paradigm emerged. Influenced by the teachings of Stanley Keleman, David Boadella, Gerda Boyenson, Peter Levine and others, the focus shifted. My therapist was having sessions with Stanley Keleman and being trained by Gerda Boyenson; and because of their influence, my therapy changed. Now, she not only commented about my outside structure, she also focused on the flow of the energy inside my body. So after my legs were tired from being against the wall, I lay on the mat while she with her hands, gave support to my head or my belly, hoping to soften the ›inner tube‹, the flow of energy from my throat through my viscera. It was during that time that my therapy stalemated and ended. I became aware that to open my heart, I needed an empathic attuned person who could resonate with me and feel what I needed somatically, emotionally and verbally.

And one morning at a conference in Montebello, I was finally able to voice my protest about being viewed as an energetic body detached from a person. My friend was practicing a technique she had learned from Peter Levine. In case you are unfamiliar with him, he spoke at our conference in Montebello a few years ago and has developed a somatic therapy for working with trauma. The technique is called: ›Opening the Four Diaphragms‹. I like this intervention; and in fact, taught it to the faculty earlier this week. When working together in the past, she had noticed that my body sometimes was able to go into what Levine calls harmonic resonance or the streamings that comprise ›The Big O‹. As she became more intent on watching my body, I wondered if she really cared about me or was more attached to producing a somatic effect. I began to cry and said to her: »Please be as interested in me as you are in my body.« She, being a sensitive therapist reached and took my hand. Later that morning Bob Lewis was addressing the entire conference at Montebello. He mentioned that he had said the same thing to his therapist: »Please be as interested in me as you are in my body«. Thanks again Bob Lewis.

At this time a third paradigm is emerging influenced by the teachings and writings of Len Carlino, David Finlay, Bob Hilton, and Bob Lewis and supported by the latest neurobiological research and investigative studies regarding the process and efficacy of psychotherapy. Research on what causes change in psychotherapy has repeatedly given us the same finding, that therapy change is occurring because of something happening in the relationship between the therapist and client. No longer is the therapist a separate objective observer reading the outside of the body or a neutral person affecting the inside.

Angela Klopstech (2002) extends Stark's (1999) model of three ways of interacting with clients and demonstrates how a body intervention can be used in these different ways. In case you are unfamiliar with Martha Stark's work, she spoke at the conference in Montebello 2001. Klopstech describes classical Bioenergetics as basically a »one person psychology«, with the therapist functioning as an observer, who interprets and provides knowledge to the client. In her words: »Over the last decade, Bioenergetic Analysis experienced a process similar to psychoanalysis, i.e., a shift towards a more relationship-oriented approach (...). This process is still much more in its infancy as compared to the shift that psychoanalysis has undergone. The relevant Bioenergetic literature is borrowing mainly from psychoanalytic publications on an ›as needed basis‹ and has not yet jelled into a coherent theoretical structure« (Klopstech 2002, p. 58). She describes working with a client who has difficulty expressing his anger to his wife, by using a typical Bioenergetic technique, hitting the cube. First, she provides a classical Bioenergetic experience, interpreting and providing knowledge to the client. Her second intervention provides an empathic curative experience, while during her third intervention, she engages in an active relational interchange.

To understand the development of these three paradigms, we must trace the history of Bioenergetics as a therapy. When discussing our theoretical roots, we begin with Reich. His theories and research included not only the domains of psychotherapy but extended beyond into the realms of energy, politics, and the weather. He was a psychoanalyst and was formulating his psychotherapy of the body and energy as a reaction against the tyranny of mentalization and words. When he focused on patterns in patients' actions, thoughts, feelings, and relationships, he was observing how they correlated with the person's body in terms of their muscular holdings and life energy. Patients' past experiences – their early attachments, childhood experiences and historical relationships – were important for understanding character. Character is the way the person relates in the present. Because he was more interested in how the patient was in the therapeutic hour and paid less attention to his patients' associations and thoughts, Reich might be described as one of the first relational psychotherapists.

Lowen picked up on Reich's middle period when he was interested in correlating psychoanalytic theory and the body. Like Reich, he was formulating his theories in reaction against the bias of verbalization, and tended to de-emphasize mental states, images, and dreams. He made some brilliant contributions to the field of psychotherapy. His classic work, *The Language of The Body* (1958) defines a character analysis in relationship to a developing body. In addition, he describes what psychological stresses, and manifestations occur, when one is living in a society providing an immense amount of stimulation at a rapid pace and judges its standard as something outside of the person's internal feelings and sense of themselves. Within the field of psychoanalysis his book on narcissism places it as a process occurring within and among all characters. This is a brilliant piece of analysis formed at least in large part by the way I think Lowen often knows his truth, not by analyzing theories, but by observing, being with and resonating to people.

And a year and a half ago at Pawling, I was about to take a walk, when Lowen called me into the room and began to talk about what he felt had been important to him in his therapy journey. He said to stay true to what you know; and for him, that has been to follow the body. He said that he had been briefly interested in Reich's concept of orgone and energy, but now he saw that as a distraction to what was truly important.

Reich and Lowen are our legacy, the roots from which we grow. What has Bioenergetics become today and how does it compare to other therapeutic modalities? An area of controversy emerging in the therapeutic literature is the role of affect and emotion. I think it is safe to say that most Bioenergetic therapists work with affect and emotional expression. When opening up somatic holding patterns, which are blocks to emotional needs, we certainly support people in their emotional expression. When we say, we help the person be with their feelings, I'm not referring to ›getting rid of feelings‹. I remember at a talk in Greece a few years ago, Lowen stood up and yelled: »Bioenergetics is not catharsis«. Catharsis is the discharge of feelings. In a character analysis certain feelings are encouraged, while at other times, affects are contained and soothed.

The role of emotions and affect are being reexamined in attachment and trauma theory. Cognitive behavioral therapists and trauma therapists work to contain and modulate affect, while therapists working in the realm of emotionally focused psychotherapy, psychoanalytic, and Bioenergetic Analysis believe that change occurs when affect is fairly high. One of the latest concepts in the field of psychotherapy comes from the literature on trauma and is used to describe the processes when patients are managing highly charged emotional and traumatic material. This is *the therapeutic window*. It is the optimal level of arousal and affect for processing traumatic material. I'll say it again. The therapeutic window is the optimal level of arousal and affect for processing traumatic material. When discussing this concept, I will be using a few terms from neurobiology. You don't need to remember them to understand the concepts.

In neurobiological research, a dichotomy between the two areas of the brain is emphasized. The limbic brain and the cortical brain are distinct in function as well as anatomical location (cortical on top of the limbic). How these two areas of the brain interact with each other varies not only between individuals, but from minute to minute within an individual. The limbic system corresponds to a phylogenetically older, unconscious, reflexive affective brain. This part of the brain processes somatosensory (external sensory material as well) non-verbal material. It is the emotional brain that develops between one to three years of life and is influenced by our early experiences with caretakers (other parts of the brain develop during this period as well. And: ›the emotional brain‹ keeps developing during a lifetime). It is the part of the brain that Bioenergetic Analysts, more than other psychotherapists work with directly (this is – to my knowledge – only a hypothesis so far; it has not been investigated so far. And besides: e.g. flooding techniques in behavior therapy probably stimulate limbic areas as well). Cortical areas, on the other hand, represent the narrative, linguistic, symbolic, and conscious brain, which is the area of primary focus in a cognitive and psychoanalytic therapy. There are connections between the two, and each can influence the other. These two areas of the brain process memory and information differently. Emotional memory of the limbic system is encoded by intense affective or sensory events such as trauma. Declarative memory is encoded in the symbolic form of language. It has been proposed by many, such as Brockman, Siegel (1999), and Schore (1997) that therapeutic change results from bringing the full capacities of the cortical brain to intense affective experiences. Basically, this has been the process of a Bioenergetic Analysis, to bring our bodily experiences into conscious awareness and full intellectual understanding. In the past we focused on the outside of the body, somatic holding patterns, and then the inside of the body and visceral feelings.

A second concept that is appearing in the literature is that bodily states are represented in the brain. Now is the time to focus on the body that lives in the mind or the *body/mind*. This term is an important concept. There has been a split in Bioenergetics between the head and the body. People have said: »Get out of your head and back into the body«. I think that the body is in the mind and will give you some research supporting this concept. The new techniques for studying the brain provide increased information about its structure and function. With the introduction of brain imaging techniques and pet scans, somatic states have been correlated with not only physical parts of the brain, but the mind has been reintroduced as an energetic system. No longer are we a mind vs. a body, but the mind and the body are one, functioning as an intricately related system transferring information regarding somatic states and processing verbal and cognitive events. Our somatosensory experiences are represented in our mind. We are born with a complete representation of our body in our brain. How do I know this? Well, let me tell you. This is really interesting research – almost as good as the ›Big O‹. Researchers at McGill University in Canada found that people born without arms and legs still feel those body parts (Melzack et al. 1997, pp. 1603–20). This means that people feel arms and legs even though they are missing at birth. The researchers conclude that the brain needs to have information about what is going to happen. It anticipates that it will be getting information from a body that has two arms and legs, and that there will be a mother with two breasts as sources of food. »The body we perceive is in large part built into our brain – it's not entirely learned«.

Our body/mind anticipates stimulation from the caretaker. It has already formed a somatosensory neural network developed to receive stimulation. That stimulation builds structure and forms our somatosensory memories. This somatosensory structure is what psychoanalysts call the unconscious. Because of this neurobiological research, analysts are now becoming aware of the importance of somatic interventions. Bioenergetic therapists have for years worked with techniques that influence these structures.

Researchers studying the mind have found that traumatic events are stored in a part of the brain called the cingulate gyrus. Traumatic experiences overwhelm the system and they remain stored in the cingulate gyrus not as memories, but as highly affective events never fully processed and organized by the system. They are stored as somatosensory experiences and feelings. This structure, the cingulate gyrus stores these highly arousing stimulating events until they can be organized by the cerebral cortex into a coherent verbal description of the event. Another part of the brain, the thalamus acts as a door between the cingulate gyrus and the cerebral cortex. The thalamus pulses at about 40 beats / minute. When the organism is in a state of trauma, somatosensory information floods the system. The thalamus is presented with more stimuli than the cerebral cortex is able to organize, so the material is routed back to the cingulate gyrus.

Trauma time is always present time. Character is now. That's why we can't »just get over it«. Organizing information about our character, information we gather through body readings and by feeling the experience in our bodies needs to be gathered in measured doses in order for this material to be passed through the thalamus and organized by the cerebral cortex. Thus, the therapeutic window is the optimal level of arousal for moving the material through. It is the amount of highly affective activating material that can be processed by a person without them flooding, dissociating or freezing. Then, the material can be transferred to the cerebral cortex where it is organized into a coherent life story; a narrative about what happened in the past, not an ongoing traumatic experience.

Let me give you an example. A young man in one of the first year training groups would report that everything was fine. When asked to elaborate by the other trainees, he became defensive and angry, saying that he had already told them how he felt. One day, I noticed that he flinched when one of the male trainers walked by. I told him what I had seen and he seemed curious about the behavior. I pointed out how his body stiffened and pulled back, almost like the beginning of the Babinsky startle reflex. I also told him I had noticed that he only reacted this way when men walked by, looming over him. When I said the words, »looming over him«, his face blanched and his eyes looked vacant. When one of the trainees asked him how he felt, he didn't answer but remained in what trauma therapists call ›frozen immobility‹, he couldn't fight or flee. Because he was already flooded, I wanted to give him time to come into the room and protect him from more input. I told him that he was safe and that he didn't have to do or say anything. I would wait for him. The vacant look in his eyes cleared. I invited him to find the parts of his body he could feel. After finding his legs and recognizing the desire to flee, he said, »My father beat me«. Again, his body stiffened and his eyes began to have a glassy appearance. I brought his attention back to the room and then slowly invited him back into his body, modulating and titrating how much he was beginning to reexperience.

He had a good therapist and by the end of the fourth year of training, he was able to talk about the physical and verbal abuse he received from his father without flooding. It was past abuse, not happening anymore. The events now exist as a coherent narrative, as memories that are stored in the cerebral cortex. He is less often flooded by body feelings of fear and shame.

Although important and necessary for healing, these psychotherapeutic issues are still within the first and second paradigm. These are processes occurring within the client, which are separate from what is being created by the therapist and client together, the third paradigm. When the relationship is included in the therapeutic analysis, the ability to influence these processes is augmented.

Let us take a look at Lowen's own biographical narrative of his therapy with Reich. The following is a description in Lowen's own words taken from the book, *Bioenergetics*.

> »Following the experience of fear when I saw my mother's face, I went through a long stretch of several months during which I made no progress. I was seeing Reich three times a week then, but I was blocked because I couldn't tell Reich my feelings about him. I wanted him to take a fatherly interest in me, not merely a therapeutic one, but knowing this was an unreasonable request, I couldn't express it. Struggling inwardly with the problem, I got nowhere. Reich seemed unaware of my conflict. Try as hard as I could to let my breathing become deeper and fuller, it just didn't work.
>
> I had been in therapy about a year when this impasse developed«.

Lowen says he was able to discharge a great amount of fear and then he hit a plateau, unable to deepen his breathing or report feelings. Now I want you to think about what you might do if you had a client in the same situation. Turn to your neighbor and talk about what intervention you might use (3 minutes).

This is what Reich did.

> »Reich suggested I quit. »Lowen«, he said, »you are unable to give in to your feelings. Why don't you give up«? His words were a sentence of doom. To give up meant the failure of all my dreams. I broke down and cried deeply. It was the first time I had sobbed since I was child. I could no longer hold back my feelings. I told Reich what I wanted from him, and he listened sympathetically« (Lowen 1975, p. 21).

This is the defining moment in Lowen's therapy. He goes on to say, that shortly after the breakdown in the therapy, Reich took a vacation. When he returned, Reich suggested that they take a break from therapy for a year. Perhaps, Lowen was hurt, when Reich left him. I wonder what Bioenergetics would have looked like as a therapy system if Reich had treated Lowen the way you would have treated your client?

Several years ago at Arles, Leslie Case gave a talk outlining the number of ways her therapists had injured her. I was sitting with my husband, a physician, during this talk. At first he looked at me and said, »She's talking here about a certain type of clients«. I said nothing but put my arm on top of his. Next he whispered rather harshly: »Well you've done that too«, referring to the number of ways Leslie had been dismissed or accused. »Of course«, I whispered back. Finally, he held his head in his hands and said, »I've hurt so many people«. I answered: »We all have«.

In the past we have been hurt in Bioenergetics and have hurt others. And unless we are willing to learn from our mistakes, we will continue to do harm and be harmed in the same ways. Lowen at one point said that he felt that Bioenergetics didn't work because people were sicker than he believed. That statement has a ring of truth to it. The belief at that time was that if the armor was removed, then the true authentic healthy self would be revealed. The problem is that armor describes the outside of the person, it is the muscular holdings one builds to defend against feelings and needs that weren't met when we were young. Armor is a surface structure.

The second paradigm shifted the focus from only looking at the outside holding patterns to inside the person. This second shift produced great contributions to the field of Bioenergetics – Stanley Keleman's classic work *Emotional Anatomy* (1985) and the work in Bodynamics on the internal tube and viscera. The findings from neurobiology and Peter Levine's work on how the brain processes trauma are all part of the second paradigm. Levine's research focusing on the brain and mind is confirming the necessity of working with non-verbal states. But how should we work with these states? If we become too enamored of the inside of the body as we have been by the outside, we will continue to harm and be harmed by our psychotherapeutic interventions.

Now that it is time for another paradigm shift, what should be the nature of this shift? Fortunately the field of somatic psychotherapy is finally producing some good researchers who are beginning to ask the question: »Does Bioenergetic therapy heal and how«? Christa Ventling (2002) conducted a terrific research study for which she won an award from *The USA Body Psychotherapy Association*. The good news is that her research validated the effectiveness of Bioenergetic Analysis.[1]

1 This replicates the results from Gudat (1997). Koemeda-Lutz et al. (2003) report preliminary positive results from a prospective study evaluating the effectiveness of body psychotherapies.

However, Ventling also discusses the following result:

> »Although we assumed that our patients would be ascribing a high efficacy to body work with regard to gaining new insights, we were disappointed in the answer, as only 56% did so. Even fewer (46%) felt that bodywork was the cause of their improved quality of life. Clearly the exact variables that are causing the overall very positive changes in BAT (*Bioenergetic Analysis*) cannot be pinpointed at this time. The theory that it is mainly the bodywork needs further investigation. We assume that the quality of the relationship between patient and therapist plays a major role and plan to study it further« (Ventling 2002, p. 21).

Let me repeat, only a little more than half of the clients reported that the body work caused them to heal and less than half reported it improved their quality of life. This is the same finding that Pamela Bell reported to us earlier in the conference when researching the effect of Bioenergetic therapy on brain wave activity. She found that while there was a small effect on brain wave activity from participating in Bioenergetic exercise classes, a masochistic patient showed a significant amount of change after a particularly expressive therapy session. Christa Ventling in her article suggests that the healing occurred in the relationship. But what part of that relationship? In the same journal Douglas Radandt (2002) tried to investigate a possible relationship between a therapist's body awareness and the strength of the therapeutic alliance. Randant found although there was a positive correlation between the therapist's awareness of his own body sensations and movements and the therapeutic alliance, it did not reach statistical significance. If the body work by the patient and the therapist's awareness of his own body are only contributing a small portion to the therapeutic outcome, what is causing therapeutic change in Bioenergetics? Parish and Eagle in the recent journal of *Psychoanalytic Psychology* (2003) say: »There seems to be an increasing consensus that therapeutic change is based not only on cognitive factors such as awareness and insight«. For psychoanalysts, awareness and insight have been the focus while for Bioenergetic Analysts, bodily awareness, physical expression as well as cognitive factors and insights have been the focus. So what is causing the change? The writers suggest that change occurs because of the nature of the relationship between patient and therapist. And again, the question is: what part of the relationship?

There has been wide recognition that patients in psychotherapy often experience strong feelings toward their therapists, transference. One useful way of understanding the therapeutic relationship, when it works well is that the therapist, at least in certain respects, as David Campbell and Bob Hilton have been telling us for years serves, as an attachment figure, as a ›secure base‹ from which the patient can explore his or her inner world. Remember, Lowen was longing for Reich to be a secure loving father, who would be interested in him. Thus, the missing elements of our study of body awareness or bodywork interventions are: empathy, attunement, and congruence. Because the therapist is aware of his own body sensations does not mean that he is attuned to what is happening within the client's body. In other words, I suspect that it is the therapist's awareness of what the client needs in terms of an attachment figure, including somatic and bodily interventions. Our ability to be empathic and attuned to the client is what is healing in the *relationship*.

Let me give you an example of body attunement. It is from the book *Seabiscuit*, the name of the most famous racehorse in American history. The story is really about the relationship between the horse, his trainer, and his jockey. Seabiscuit is about to race against War Admiral. The country has been waiting several years for this match to occur. Even President Roosevelt is listening on the radio and won't let his advisors enter the room until the race is finished. Seabiscuit is a short stocky less favored horse. They are approaching the track to begin the race.

> »War Admiral walked up the track first, twirling and bobbing. Blunt-bodied Seabiscuit plodded along behind, head down. He looked up once, scanned the crowd, then lowered his head again« (Hillenbrand 2002, p. 268).

Let's pause a minute here. Ask yourself: What do you think Seabiscuit is feeling?

Here is what people at the time who actually saw Seabiscuit thought he was feeling.

> »One witness compared him to a milk-truck horse. Shirley Povich of the Washington Post thought he exhibited ›complete and colossal indifference‹«.

This is what his jockey says about him.

> »The appearance was deceiving. Woolf could feel it. In post parades he was accustomed to the smooth levelness of Seabiscuit's walk, the gentle gait of a horse who puts his hooves down carefully. But this day Woolf felt something new, a gathering beneath him, something springlike. The horse was coiling up«.

Woolf was sensing something happening inside the horse that a person reading the horse's body language from outside can't know. He was exploring his ›felt sense‹, and it was different from what he saw when drawing conclusions from observations about the horse's external body language.

The current research utilizing brain imaging is finding that this somatic empathic attunement appears to be necessary for developing attachment in infants and for any therapy process. This research, which has been summarized by Alan Schore and others points to the importance of the right brain in attachment, trauma, and integrating emotional experiences. They have found that what is healing in psychotherapy is the relationship, and much of what transpires between the therapist and client is transmitted to the occipital cortex and is unconscious both to the client and the therapist. This part of the brain develops between the ages of one to three years of age, again (schizoid to rigid), but most dramatically in the first few months. This means that the memories stored there are nonverbal and comprise implicit memory, the same kind of memory that is used for such functions like riding a bicycle or knitting. These are body memories. We don't have a verbal description of the steps needed each time we get on a bicycle or knit. Even if we haven't ridden a bike or picked up knitting or crochet needles for years, we still remember how to do it.

An experience from my own life illustrates how these memories function. I'm quoting from my article in the recent IIBA journal on research.

> »I had the privilege of having my baby at home, so the morning after Myrrhia's birth I turned on the radio while she nursed. Music passionately delivered by a gospel choir mirrored the joy I felt for having such a beautiful being in my arms and I began dancing. Previous to her birth, I had never listened much to gospel music and had certainly never danced to it. I found myself moving to this music during the first three years of her babyhood and even purchased a couple of albums.

> Many years later, when Myrrhia was 8-years-old, she and I were having tea with my Aunt Barbara. My aunt told me that the black woman, Helen Bell who helped care for me the first four years of my life was the lead person in the gospel church. Every Sunday she would dance down the aisles leading her congregation. She loved gospel music and must have danced, holding the baby Helen (me) in her arms. So, although I didn't know that Helen Bell went to church or danced, my body had stored memories of that experience. Holding my baby released memories of my own infancy, which until Aunt Barbara had told me about, I didn't know had been my experience.
>
> These early attachment experiences are stored in our limbic brain as a prototype for relationships« (Resneck-Sannes 2002, pp. 113–114).

We aren't able to retrieve these memories by our usual method of verbal or even visual recall. They are stored as somatic impressions drawing us to certain relationships. A certain behavior emerged, dancing to gospel music triggered by the birth of my daughter. Dancing is a somatosensory behavior which mirrored an experience from my infancy of which I have no conscious memory.

So that explains implicit memory, but I'm discussing something beyond memory. I'm talking about a communication between two minds, an empathic attunement. Here is another example straight from the Bioenergetic mat. At lunch one day I was discussing with a colleague of mine, Tom, the importance of understanding the difference between placing a hand under or on top of the hand or foot of a client. He described a situation while working with a man on the mat. The man had placed his hand on his chest, and Tom placed his hand over his client's hand. Tom then had the sense that he needed to place his hand on the man's chest and have the man place his hand on top of his. We discussed the differences between the two interventions: support vs. being trapped, being held vs. being held down, but the key here is that Tom's mind/body knew what was the right thing to do.

When the therapist is in resonance with his client, then he can present material that stimulates or soothes. By titrating the amount of material presented the therapist prevents the client from being over-whelmed, dysregulated and at worst re-traumatized. An empathic therapist is neither understimulating (too removed, neutral, not there), nor over-stimulating (not modulating the material) to prevent the client from flooding, dissociating or splitting off. When our clients are over-charged and over-stimulated, we need to calm and contain our own energy. The therapist needs to be attuned such that the material is within the therapeutic window, enabling it to be passed through the thalamus to the cerebral cortex.

Our body interventions should become an invitation for the client to explore somatically (sensate) feelings, meanings, imagistic representations, and internal object representations. We then become the mirroring, empathic, attuned other that hopefully will begin to live inside our client's body/mind and support them in being who they are: vulnerable, needy, scared, loving, hard, angry, punishing, resentful, sadistic, victim, little child who wants to be rescued.

One of the important aspects of teaching character analysis is to train Bioenergetic therapists in this kind of body empathy. A reading of the body should lead to a greater understanding of the client's issues, not only intellectually but to trigger an empathic response and adjustment in our own bodies. The neurobiological research, the psychoanalytic journals, the emotionally focused therapy articles, they are all talking about the importance of somatic attunement for processing emotionally laden material. Yet, none of this literature is mentioning the word Bioenergetics or referring to our arsenal of techniques and interventions. We can titrate, modulate in a way that other analytic and cognitive behavioral therapists are unable. Our knowledge of breath, of grounding, of ways to form somatic and energetic boundaries, and our knowledge of affect containment enables us to be sensitive to flooding. When I have clients who are over-charged or suffering from chronic illnesses resulting from an over-reactive immune system, like fibromyalgia or chronic fatigue, my physical contact is different from when I am trying to open a block. In both cases my touch is firm. However, when clients are highly activated, I try to maintain a state of grounded stillness. I slowly and gently make contact, waiting for my hand to feel their pulsation. This is different from when I am opening a block. Then, I ground by allowing my own breath to deepen and my charge to build. I contact the body part that needs to release, waiting for the area of holding to soften, inviting me in deeper, as deep as the body allows. None of this is new to you. We learn about different kinds of touch and contact the first year of training.

I recently experienced a painful bout of sciatica. When the nerves of my back were inflamed, I sadly experienced how few body workers are aware of attuned contact. Before this bout of sciatica, I used to ask people to stand on my back, including Jim Miller (all three hundred pounds of him). When the nerves of my spine were inflamed, I needed a gentle touch. I couldn't get a massage therapist to understand how to touch me without putting charge into my body.

I meet with a group of therapists twice a year to work on ourselves. Before our meeting I had a fantasy of being gently held. Without me needing to ask, Virginia Hilton offered to hold me. Her touch was sensitive and present, yet not activating, invasive or demanding. Bioenergetic Analysts have these skills and no one knows. There have been few books written and until recently, very little research. What a shame.

Finally, one more change needs to occur in the practice of Bioenergetic Analysis. As I mentioned before, the concept has been that the body is the access to the unconscious. By enabling clients to be aware of their somatic holding patterns, the energy will flow freely through the body in a harmonic wave. This has been the thinking of all the somatic therapies so far. As I mentioned before, it is a non-relational theory. The research has been showing for years that clients report that neither insight nor body interventions heal by themselves. I think the body interventions are necessary but not sufficient for healing. I'm not saying that our somatic interventions should be discarded. Quite the contrary, they must occur in the context of an attuned, empathic relationship. This means that the therapist must no longer be separate from the client, but now must enter the room as a human being.

For instance, let's address the issue of anger. When clients hit the cube, it is a means for them to recognize the holding patterns of anger in their body and to identify with the emotion and the body sensations. The goal of hitting is not to »get rid of feelings« as so often has been the confusion of therapists; nor is it a way of dealing with resistance in the therapy. Hitting the cube is to enable the client to connect with the feeling of anger and the muscles used to either hold back or express it.

However, when we have injured a client and they are angry with us, we don't only direct them to hit a cube. We are the ones who need to be able to say, »I'm sorry« and repair the damage we inadvertently or necessarily caused. Of course, we don't want to hurt people, but we do. It is the reparation of these moments of therapeutic disruption that lead to healing. Ruptures and repair are part of the therapy process. A character analysis, a true relational therapy recognizes that the therapist has to be present for all of the client's feelings – love, anger, rage, sexuality, and resistance. Hitting is important for a client to recognize anger, the holding in the back and the arms. But a cube can't say »I'm sorry«. We need to say »I'm sorry«.

Let me give you an example from my own practice. A woman I have been seeing for several years entered my office on the verge of tears. She is a sophisticated psychotherapist, has good analytic skills which she uses defensively to hide her hurt and vulnerability. Although she wasn't directly accusing me, she was telling me that I hadn't stayed focused on her vulnerable issues. She went on to say that the night before, while talking to her partner, she became so frustrated that her attempt to push the cat off of the bed became a kick. Although she was surprised and shocked by her aggression, the client was more upset that her partner didn't remain interested in her feelings; and instead wanted to process her shock about the physical aggression used on the cat. She then told me of all the ways she could not be comforted, didn't believe people's empathy. She continued saying that in our therapy she had avoided these painful feelings which allowed her to be vulnerable by analyzing others. I had a fantasy of offering her my hand to hold, which I was aware she would probably reject. However, I felt that it was important that I make the offer. As I expected, she told me that it wasn't enough. She then asked why she felt bad and couldn't accept my offer. Once again, she was avoiding difficult feelings by analyzing her needs and motives. Although in the past I had colluded with her in avoiding these issues, this time I answered: »I'm sorry for disrupting your expression by offering my hand. I'm also sorry for in the past when I explored your needing to ask why. But this time, I don't care why. I just want to be here with you. I don't even care if I do it right, I just want to be here with you«. She started to cry and then began analyzing her body sensations, why her partner couldn't give that response. I stopped her and just said, »I'm sorry that I let you avoid these feelings in the past, but I am with you now«. She began to sob deeply. I felt that I was saying »I'm sorry« for the missed opportunities to comfort her and for all of the people who missed comforting her. It was more important to repair those missed moments than to have the ›correct somatic intervention‹.

Now I will talk about the future by asking: What is our standing in the therapeutic community now and what is possible for us? First, do you know what is considered the cutting edge of psychotherapeutic practice today? Cognitive Behavioral therapy. Why? Because they have research studies validating the efficacy of their approach. Investigators from the University of Northern Iowa surveyed 425 clinical psychologists, and 254 of them reported having experienced depression. Although 53% of the depressed therapists said they employ primarily cognitive-behavioral methods in their practices, 40% chose psychodynamic therapy for their own treatment. The second most popular modality they sought was Gestalt (19%). Only 12% sought cognitive behavioral therapy. So while insurance companies in the U.S. tend to reimburse for cognitive behavioral interventions, that is not the modality that clinicians are choosing for themselves when they need help (Parish & Eagle 2003).

Why aren't they choosing Bioenergetics? It's not even mentioned as a possible choice of intervention. Like psychoanalysis and cognitive behavioral therapy, we need to develop a literary tradition espousing the interventions that are specific to Bioenergetic Analysis. We need to concentrate on those interventions that heal and try to localize the ingredients, both active and passive that contribute to therapeutic change. I would like you for a moment to consider the following remarks that were made during a panel discussion at the 2002 meeting of the psychoanalytic society. (Kirsner, D. 2001) Present on the panel were some of the most well known analysts of our time. Douglas Kirsner began with a highly critical view of the ›unwarranted claims to knowledge‹ made by analysts in the absence of scientific support. Otto Kernberg urged the development of clear standards for training. The need to develop research skills as a part of training he called an ›essential task‹. Robert Wallerstein discussed the organizational structure of institutes and their curricula. Feeling that psychoanalysis must avail itself of developments in allied fields, such as cognitive sciences, he supported the move of institutes into academic settings ›in order to survive‹.

We, Bioenergetic Analysts are also faced with the knowledge that if we wish to become members of the larger therapeutic community, then we must gear our research and theory to what is considered the cutting edge of practice today. In so doing, do we lose what is essential to a Bioenergetic practice? Or, by joining with the larger community are we incorporating effective therapeutic techniques, enhancing our knowledge base and becoming a major force in the community at large? If we don't join, I'm afraid that we are in danger of becoming an esoteric therapeutic community that dissolves into the mists like Avalon and King Arthur's knights of the round table, an idealized memory in the minds of a select few.

This time in history is an especially fortuitous one for somatic psychotherapies. We have been aware that trauma is stored in the body. Developmental trauma is stored there. In fact, all of the latest research points to a body psychotherapy. Schore proposes that ›primitive mental states‹ are more precisely characterized as ›psychobiological states‹. The field of psychotherapy is acknowledging that the focus of therapy must shift from cognitions, images, and dreams to include non-verbal somatic states. Bioenergetic Analysts are attuned to these states and deep somatic experiences. The time is now for us to join with other analytic and trauma therapists, not only to learn what they have to offer but to inform and to teach them that we know how to regulate somatic states. We should be writing articles for other journals, like *The USA Body Psychotherapy Journal* as well as for traditional psychoanalytic and academic journals. We need to be teaching in academic settings and providing support for students engaging in research. It is imperative that we join with and support other therapy organizations both where we live and in the larger psychotherapy community. We can be informative and even teach them a few things by sharing our ideas, letting them know that we have interventions and theories that are helpful to and consistent with the way they are doing therapy. Lowen was our spokesperson, writing books and demonstrating Bioenergetic practice at large conferences. He has retired and we need to step forward and take his place. We have a great deal to offer to the psychotherapeutic community and now is the time.

References

Brockman, R. (1998): A map of the mind: Toward a science of Psychotherapy, Madison, Ct. (Psychosocial Press).

Brockman, R.. (2001): Toward a Neurobiology of the Unconscious. Journal of the American Academy of Psychoanalysis and Dynamic Psychiatry 29(4), 601–615.

Gudat, U. (1997): Bioenergetische Analyse als ambulante Psychotherapie – Anwendungsbereiche und Wirkungen. Psychotherapie Forum 5, 28–37.

Hillenbrand, L. (2002): Seabuiscuit – An American Legend. New York (The Ballantine Publishing Group).

Keleman, S. (1985): Emotional Anatomy. Berkeley, California (Center Press).

Kirsner, D. (2001): The Future of Psychoanalytic Institutes – A Dialogue. Psychoanalytic Psychologist, 18(2),195–212.

Klopstech. A. (2002): Modelle therapeutischen Handelns: Der psychoanalytische und der bioenergetische Weg. In: Koemeda-Lutz, M. (Hg.) Körperpsychotherapie – Bioenergetische Konzepte im Wandel. Basel (Schwabe Verlag). Engl.: The Bioenergetic Use of a Psychoanalytic Conception of Cure. Bioenergetic Analysis. The Clinical Journal of the International Institute for Bioenergetic Analysis, 11 (1) 55–66.

Koemeda-Lutz M., Kaschke M., Revenstorf D., Scherrmann T., Weiss, H. & Soeder U. (2003): Zwischenergebnisse zur Wirksamkeit von ambulanten Körperpsychotheapien. Eine Multicenter-Studie in Deutschland und der Schweiz. Psychotherapie Forum 11 (2) 70–79.

Engl.: Preliminary Results Concerning the Effectiveness of Body-Psychotherapies in Outpatient Settings – A Multi-Center Study in Germany and Switzerland (www.eabp.org).

Lowen, A. (1958): The Language of the Body. New York (Collier Books).

Lowen, A. (1975): Bioenergetics. New York (Penguin Books).

Lowen, A. (1983): Narcissism. New York (Macmillan Publishing Co.).

Melzack, I., Lacroix, R. & Schultz,G. (1997): Phantom limbs in people with congenital limb deficiency or amputation in early childhood. Brain 120, 1603–20.

Parish, M. & Eagle, M. (2003): Attachment to the therapist. Psychoanalytic Psychology 20 (2) 271–286.

Radandt, D. (2002): Therapist's Body Awareness and Strength of the Therapeutic Alliance. The USA Body Psychotherapy Journal, 52–62.

Schore, A.N. (1997): A century after Freud's Project: Is a rapprochement between psychoanalysis and neurobiology at hand? Journal of the American Psychoanalytic Association, 45, 841–867.

Siegel, D.J. (1999): The developing mind: Toward a neurobiology of interpersonal experience. New York (Guilford Press).

Stark, M. (1999): Modes of Therapeutic Action. Northvale N.J. (Jason Aronson).

Ventling, C. (2002): Efficacy of Bioenergetic Therapies and Stability of the Therapeutic Result: A Retrospective Investigation. The USA Body. Psychotherapy Journal, 5–27.

Helen Resneck-Sannes, Ph.D.,
216 Suburbia Avenue,
Santa Cruz, CA, 95062, USA,
E-mail: HelenRS@aol.com

Emotional Inhibition and Disease

Harald C. Traue, Russell M. Deighton and Petra Ritschi

The assertion that suppressed feelings are dangerous for health is a crucial component of non-professional disease theories. »Due to the fact that I swallow everything, my stomach aches all the time« is for example, such a self-diagnosis. These assumptions have their source in a long scientific tradition. William James (1890), the philosopher and founder of empirical psychology, was probably the first of the academic psychologists to take the view that suppressed feelings can cause physical diseases, worry and inner restlessness. But William James, who also wrote about religious issues, surely knew psalm 32 which says: »When I kept silence, my bones waxed old through my roaring all the day long«. He realized that the assumption that emotional suppression has a health endangering effect was a hypothesis of historic validity. As is well known, a few years later it was Sigmund Freud (1904/1905, 1942, p. 240) who used similar words in an analysis of hysteria concerning suppressed emotions: »He that has eyes to see and ears to hear may convince himself that no mortal can keep a secret. If his lips are silent, he chatters with his fingertips; betrayal oozes out of him at every pore«.

Wilhelm Reich (1933) considered, what he called muscular armoring to be a physical manifestation of repression and suppression in the form of muscular activity used to prevent suppressed emotional stimuli from being transformed into action. Thus, he considered suppressive processes to be relevant to numerous, particularly psychosomatic diseases. In 1935, Helen Flanders Dunbar published many case studies in which she described emotional causes that, in her opinion, were specifically connected with physical diseases. Franz Alexander (1950) tried to describe in a more physiological way in his standard work of »Psychosomatic Medicine« the consequences of blocking emotions as the central cause of psychosomatic diseases. A huge field of research including many different methods and empirical articles (see the following monographs and anthologies: Traue & Pennebaker 1993; Pennebaker 1995; Vingerhoets et al. 1997; Traue 1998) have arisen from the above-mentioned historical roots. Accordingly, in this field of research no one asks *if* the inhibition of feelings has a harmful effect on human organisms, but rather *why and how* structural, physiological, endocrine, immunological or subjective disease processes are connected with the processing of emotions and particularly their inhibition.

Theoretical aspects of emotional behavior

About twenty years ago it became apparent that research on emotions was lacking in the field of psychology. By this time Bruce W. Heller (1983, p. 190), criticizing the behavioral and cognitive dominance in the field, lamented ironically that Descartes did not say: »I feel therefore I am«, but preferred the thinking process and thus introduced a philosophy according to which emotions were less important than cognitions. He assumed also that it would be difficult to objectify emotions for empirical and experimental research; and that therefore, it would be better to avoid them. The horse of emotionality disappeared from the stable for centuries. It was ignored that emotions are strongly influenced by thoughts and vice versa, and that both processes are inseparably connected with each other.

Today, this is no longer the case. Current theories assert that emotions represent a complex structure composed of the following different elements:

1) Expressiveness of facial expressions, gestures and the whole body
2) Cognitive assessment of internal and external stimuli
3) Physiological and endocrine activation
4) A cognitive plan of action and an action tendency
5) Subjective experience and linguistic representation

Just as a river changes its course and flow over time, when discussing the phenomenology of emotions, the chronological process has to be considered. Emotions are a process. They separate the behavioral reaction from its stimulus by replacing fixed, reflex-like stimulus-response patterns or instinctive, innate trigger mechanisms with flexible behavioral responses. By doing so, fixed reflexive responses are replaced by cognitive appraisal processes of stimuli and situations. Especially the facial expression component of emotional behavior is a central part of interpreting which possible action tendencies and intentions of the individual will be communicated into his social environment. Only by doing so, does emotional behavior gain its regulating function not only within but also between individuals. Based on the described complexity of emotions and their process, functions and modes of function can be derived from emotions that enable us to classify the role of emotional inhibition (see Traue 1998 and 1999).

Emotions give subjective meaning

Emotions are a reaction to situations and give these situations personally relevant meaning. Here, situations are to be considered in a broad sense and comprise external (physical, social and informational) and internal (interoceptive and mental) stimulus patterns. For some stimulus patterns the emotional meanings are more standardized, i.e. more phylogenetically determined, than for others. However, some complex or ambiguous situations can only be assessed emotionally by a cognitive analysis. When intense stimulating events occur during traumatic experiences the possibility of cognitive assessment can be strongly reduced.

Emotions aid communication

Emotions help individuals adapt to their environment. The emotional structures and functions have developed in an evolutionary process, which spans not only the evolution of the nervous system, but also human social life. Although phylogenetically newer structures override older cerebral structures, they do not completely neutralize their function. Therefore, emotional behavior is based on vital, meaningful reactions that are experienced directly and contain a strong impulse to act. This urge to act can only be controlled to a certain extent. Since emotional processing has developed phylogenetically in step with human social life, the existence of a human being depends on the emotional expressiveness of its fellow human beings.

Emotional behavior is based on neurobiological structures

The entire central and peripheral nervous system is involved in emotional processes, as mental functions are involved in emotional experience via perception, attention, activation, consciousness and language. However, the neurobiological structures that are host to these functions can contribute to very specific aspects of emotional experience. Part of the central nervous structure known as the limbic system is mostly important for the processing of discrete emotions. The limbic system integrates sensory input and information from the cortex into emotional units. Recent studies emphasize that sensory information can be processed more rapidly via thalamic circuits within the amygdala than within the cortex itself. This means that certain stimuli can lead to emotional reactions without being processed consciously. The fact that the quality of emotional reaction depends on neurobiological structures is also reflected in the predominance of negative emotions that are obviously more necessary for the survival of human beings than positive emotions such as curiosity, joy and love.

Emotions can be both a process and a state

Emotions are mainly produced when information is processed. Processing of outer stimuli patterns is structured hierarchically from sensation to cognition. Emotions can also arise from inner stimuli (e.g. fantasies, ideas or memories). Since inner stimuli always contain emotional information, emotions are directly produced. Thus emotions can always be reproduced by memory independently of when they first occurred in a person's life.

Emotions are physical and mental

Emotional processes correspond directly with central, motor and autonomic nervous activity, central regulations being more important than peripheral feedback. Theoretically this derives from the communicative function of emotional processes. Empirical evidence for this comes from the stability and inter-individual agreement about emotional expressive behavior and autonomic nervous correlates. Endocrine and immunological reaction patterns differentiate between positive and negative emotions but not within these two emotional classes.

Emotional behavior is subject to self-regulation

The control of emotional reactions by suppression or inhibition has a stronger effect on motor behavior, especially expressive emotional behavior, than on the other components of emotion, and modulates it qualitatively and quantitatively. Even socio-cognitive processes have substantial influence on this component of emotion. Secondary emotions such as shame and guilt depend on an individual's capacity to anticipate the consequences of his or her behavior or emotional reaction.

The historical roots of the term: »Inhibition«

Before we turn to the inhibition of emotions, a short outline of the term »inhibition«in modern scientific history should be given. Several years ago the scientific historian, Roger Smith, professor at the Institute for Scientific History at Lancaster University, discussed in his impressive book »Inhibition« (1992) the scientific origin of the term. Smith maintains that inhibition is a central issue permeating the arts, social science and scientific theories and that within a systemic conception of human self-regulation it is fundamental. At the end of the 19th century, there was a shift from biological models of body and soul to systemic theories of human regulation. Before that, the term inhibition was used in the sense of suppression as a crucial element to the establishment of hierarchical orders in social structures, as well as the power the soul has over the body. In C.S.Sherrington's (born in 1857) neurophysiology, I. P. Pavlov's (born in 1849) theory of the higher nervous system and S. Freud's (born in 1856) psychoanalysis the term inhibition played a central role. These three experts were not only contemporaries, they also had training in experimental research and started their research work at a time in which important discoveries were made in the field of neurophysiology.

The three scientists Sherrington, Pavlov and Freud developed the concept of inhibition in different scientific contexts. These contexts have in common that they postulate activating and inhibiting forces and that they describe regulating mechanisms of equilibrium or homeostasis. The idea of adapting the individual to different environmental conditions and the idea of communication between partial and whole systems is part of these contexts. A dominance of inhibiting influences on a neuronal, central-nervous or mental level is considered to be dysfunctional. The physiological theory of inhibition has been applied to general psychological and social concepts. These initially theoretical (and empirically based) assumptions have been popularized and transformed, so that people with dysfunctional regulation have been characterized as neurotic, psychotic and physically ill. Hence, even in colloquial »theories« the inhibited type of person is considered to be socially disturbed, unimaginative in his intellectual world, deviant in his behavior and prone to psychosomatic disorders.

The inhibition of emotions

In the Western cultural tradition, actions based on feelings are disparaged. Soon after birth, parents try to teach their children the culturally appropriate manner of dealing with feelings. Parental advisory books are full of suggestions of how to make infants give up their utterances of displeasure. These books more or less say that »the whining little ones« should show their feelings the way the adults think it to be appropriate. The fact that a baby cries when she or he is hungry is accepted. A baby's protest without being hungry is not so easily accepted, and can be very annoying, especially at night, when parents want to sleep. By three years of age, parents expect their children not to refuse to go to preschool, because they would rather stay with their parents. Later, children learn not to destroy other children's toys, not to scratch cars, not to use any physical violence in discussions. In short, they learn to regulate their feelings on their own.

As young human beings grow up, they will find their emotional needs and expressions in conflict with their social group and learn to control their emotions by means of anticipating positive and negative consequences of their expression. Some people succeed in this emotional self-control – i.e. in the harmonization of personal motives and their personal and cultural value system – and others do not or are less successful. Emotional self-control that serves social life within a group can have negative consequences for an individual as the inhibition of feelings has its price. In this chapter, the way in which inhibited emotionality negatively affects individual health is discussed.

Since there is no golden standard of emotional self-control for human social life, a number of questions arise. 1) Where do the rules for emotional behavior in a given social community originate? 2) Who decides which emotional expression is appropriate and which is not? 3) What changes may have occurred in the course of history?

With a critical view on the social traditions of emotional expression, Stephan L. Chorover writes in his book »From Genesis to Genocide« that only certain human beings are always in a position to carry out manipulations of their own emotions, that these manipulations are always made in a social context and that these manipulations are often used to regulate the behavior of other human beings (1979, p. 16). In this sense emotional inhibition can be part of a general behavior strategy. There is very likely a considerable social inequality with regard to emotional inhibition.

Civilization and commercialization of feelings

Emotional control is always effected in a social context defined by historical, political and social conditions. Elias (1936) analyzed the social changes of dealing with emotions, covering the historical epoch between the Middle Ages and Modernity. One of the basic ideas of his inspiring theory discusses the wounds that can be caused by the shift of interpersonal emotional expressiveness to an implosion back into the individual self. Part of the tensions and passions that in former times directly burst into an interpersonal fight, nowadays have to be managed by and within the individual. While drives and passionate affect may no longer manifest in the external world, they are nonetheless quite often fighting, not less violently, within the individual. This semi-automatic internal struggle does not always have a happy ending. The self-transformation that life in our society requires does not always lead to a new equilibrium in the conflictual world of drives.

Norbert Elias (1936, p. 330 f.) formulates three central arguments concerning emotional self-control:

1) The more the accumulation of political and economic power increases, the more the expression of emotional behavior is restricted.
2) Politeness as a form of emotionally controlled behavior proliferated from nobility to the general public as a sign of social and political suppression. Table manners and living traditions changed concomitantly with the control of aggressiveness while thresholds for shame declined considerably. Roaring, hitting, screaming and natural signs of digestion such as farting, belching and spitting were progressively considered indecent. Due to the internalization of these new rules of behavior, control and suppression shifted from external to internal exertion.
3) The process of increasing affect control sharpened the separation of private and public worlds and may have reached its temporary pinnacle in present middle-class society. Bath and sleeping rooms have become private so that many emotions can only be experienced and lived within these very restricted areas. While, for example, in the Middle Ages, common bath and sleeping rooms were the rule, they are nowadays rather the exception.

Wouters (1986) asserts that diminished social barriers between persons and groups of persons require increased self-control within social life, and that children, although they rarely have an authoritarian upbringing which teaches them fixed limits, will later be expected to exert extremely high self-control.

The same amount of emotional control a society generally requires from its members will be required in stress reactions. Thus, the availability of psychotropic drugs and psychotherapeutic interventions such as meditation, relaxation, cognitive therapy and hypnosis, which can cushion or reduce emotional reactions, can all be interpreted as signs for the necessity of emotional inhibition. In Germany, for example, general practitioners prescribe about one package of psychotropic drugs per inhabitant per year.

In the fifties, the social scientist C. Wright Mills realized that people were becoming more and more absorbed by the world of labor: »The part of their professional life in which they could act »freely« using their own personality is now organized as well and transformed to a living but at the same time obsequious instrument for distributing the freight« (1956, p. 45). During 150 years of industrialization, labor was dominated by the production of goods more than today where the focus increasingly is on business and rendered services. However, the world of labor is now more than ever interested in subordinating or exploiting formerly private aspects of the personality of the working people, whose individual and private feelings get commercialized. This commercialization concerns the use of feelings for profit as well as the control of feelings.

Many settings for work and sometimes even for life are more or less hierarchically structured and function according to governmental control systems including rules which have been set up by authorities and which have to be followed by subordinates. Most institutions follow this scheme even if from time to time attempts are made to change them into so-called person-centered systems. Especially in times of economic crises, there is a tendency to break the rules, normally firmly established in bureaucracy. Increased control over emotions and communication among subordinate employees is supposed to also affect their creativity, thus causing losses to the institution. Even if the consequences of releasing dynamic working power are often drastic, e.g. when complete management structures are dissolved, the real power structure and hierarchies between enterprises and subordinate employees or superiors and subordinates remain untouched. These changes often veil the conflict of interests and the power structure. Such conditions do not help individuals to deal with their own and other persons' feelings.

The most important rules in governmental control systems and hierarchical structures are:

1) Feelings of proprietors and superiors are more important than those of subordinates. The feelings of these persons have to be thoroughly observed, analyzed and recognized, and have to be taken care of.

An average person's feelings are less important and must be controlled. Their open expression could be harmful and at the risk of one's safety.

These rules also apply to institutions which are proud of their liberalism. To tolerate the emotional behavior of higher ranking persons during professional debates requires lower ranking people to suppress their own feelings of frustration and anger. Without being able to come up with numbers, we are convinced that this emotional labor contributes considerably to the stress of our working life.

Another aspect of controlling one's feelings in the context of labor has to be mentioned. Arlie Hochschild examined the emotional labor in different private and professional spheres of life, especially those of stewardesses and tax collectors. Both professional groups are conspicuously characterized by a specific use of feelings and emotional labor in their work. In training syllabuses of these professions, trainees are systematically taught how to use their feelings. Hochschild sociologically defines emotional labor as a management of feelings, aiming at the formation of a publicly presentable body and facial expression and the suppression of undesirable facial expressions (Hochschild 1983).

Emotional labor »requires the showing and suppressing of feelings in order to preserve the outer attitude which has the desired effect on other persons« – this concerns the desired positive effects on flight passengers and the desired negative effects such as inducing fear in subjects regarding taxation. As a result of her study, Hochschild confirms that emotional labor is increasing in almost all professions of social, administrative and commercial services and that due to this fact, a new dimension of alienating human beings from the products and results of their own work is arising. Based on self-presentations in detailed interviews Hochschild formed four groups with different strategies of emotional labor: (1) Members of the *instrumentally oriented group* claim to be actively acting persons who use feelings in their professions, but although they use their feeling instrumentally they do not believe that their personality would really change. (2) Members of the second group report themselves as *adapted to their own emotionality*. They express situation-specific feelings but keep their real feelings private. (3) A third group of persons observes a change of their emotional behavior under the influence of emotional labor. Hochschild coined the term *emotionally deformed group* for them. They gradually adapt to the professional demands. (4) The forth group finally adopts an *active adaptation* with respect to the professional demands of their job. According to the situation they try to change, to suppress their feelings or to »really« create necessary feelings.

The term of emotional labor especially applies to the third and forth group. Here, most personal deformations and the highest stress caused by the management of feelings arise. As emotional workers, human beings are not only alienated from the direct results of their own work but also from themselves, as nothing in one's inner emotional life is more directly connected to one's own personality than personal feelings. Emotional labor in commercial and social services and social care is potentially effective and professional since nobody wants to interact with grumpy people. But what is the price for this emotional labor when inner tensions grow to cope with the professional demands on emotional self-control?

Another indicator of an increasing commercialization of human emotionality, particularly in western neo-capitalistic countries, is that real feelings become a scarce interpersonal good. Never before have there been so many offers from psychological experts to help fellow human beings to get in contact with themselves and with their own authentic feelings. These offers refer to their professional as well as to their private life. They emanate from the experience that the manipulation of emotions exacts the high social price of an increasing distance between the individual and his emotional self. It is true that emotional labor is necessary for human social life, but emotions should not be at the mercy of commercialization. To the extent that this commercialization is spreading, the experience and sharing of authentic feelings will be forced back and fade out more and more from interpersonal everyday life.

Individual differences in the inhibition of emotions

Persons differ considerably in the extent of their expressive emotional behavior. This behavior fulfills different functions: Expressive behavior serves as an interpersonal signal system which is used to communicate emotional evaluations of situations to the social environment. It is considerably involved in regulating social behavior. Facial feedback to expressive behavior provides essential information for the evaluation of situations. If expressive behavior is inhibited, the regulation of social behavior is disturbed and the individual is deprived from an essential source of information for evaluating situations. Studies conducted from different perspectives show that inhibited emotional behavior has to be considered a risk factor for the origin and maintenance of psychosomatic disorders.

It is a constituent factor of a model of health and illness which describes the bio-psychosocial interactions between emotional inhibition and disorders in health as pathways (see also Traue 1998). Here, the inhibition of emotional behavior is classified in different types which, depending on the intensity of the emotional disorder, influence the course of diseases.

Typology of emotional inhibition

The inhibition of emotional behavior is a complex action which cannot be reduced to a simple process since emotional behavior itself is very complex. According to Kagan et al. (1988) emotional inhibition is based on a genetic tendency but socialization considerably modulates the development of emotionality, especially with regard to expressive behavior. Finally cognition arising from dealing with stressful situations has to be integrated into a theory of the interrelation of inhibition and disease, as emotional action is dependent on cognitive processes, and the central-nervous representation of self-concepts and situations is mediated cognitively. The connections between inhibited emotionality and disease processes are presented by a model of health and illness which describes neurobiological, socio-behavioral and cognitive pathways between emotional inhibition and disease. Four types of emotional inhibition can be distinguished (Traue 1998, Traue & Deighton 2000, Traue 2001):[1]

1) Genetic inhibition
2) Repressive inhibition
3) Suppressive inhibition and
4) Deceptive inhibition

GENETIC INHIBITION of emotional expressiveness describes avoidance behavior, social retreat and fear of strangers. The assumption of a genetically determined inhibition is based on the observation of children at different developmental stages who exhibit considerable individual differences in emotional expressive behavior which correlate with autonomic hyper-reactivity (Field

[1] For more detailed information on the presentation of emotional implosion see Traue (1998) and Traue et al. (1997).

et al. 1982). Confronted with unfamiliar situations and novel environmental stimuli little children show clear differences in behavior. About 15–20% of healthy children between the age of 1 and 2 years are afraid of new situations, avoid new stimuli, and are described as behaviorally inhibited. About 25–30% show the opposite pattern, and are described as uninhibited. The neurobiological basis of these behavioral tendencies is analyzed more thoroughly in the next section. According to Kagan a great proportion of inhibited behavior is inherited. However, the older these children grow, the smaller the genetic influence on emotional expressiveness becomes. Furthermore it has been shown that there is a higher heritability factor in the group of extremely inhibited children, so the more extreme the inhibition, the bigger the biological basis of behavior.

Inhibited persons are also described as shy. Experts talk about genetic inhibition when someone is longing for personal contact but is inhibited, and not when someone is tired, uninterested or lazy and is therefore not seeking contact. It is not a matter of active contact avoidance, as this would be attained by different behavior, but rather passive avoidance: Persons with genetic inhibition may find nonsocial situations attractive and will avoid personal contact due to their fear of punishment or anticipation of frustration.

Genetic inhibition can be observed in about 10–15% of all infants within the first two years of their life and is considered to be a characteristic which becomes more and more stable when they grow older. Inhibited children and young persons show special neurobiological characteristics. Inhibited behavior, which in its origin is genetically determined, interacts with conditioning and stress and can thus be intensified or reduced by conditions in the environment. If children are expressively inhibited in the first months of their life, they will have problems in the relationship to their caregivers. Thus, it is very likely that these children will experience a certain lack of social care and less positive responses to their behavior.

REPRESSIVE INHIBITION of emotional behavior occurs when a person cannot completely experience or tolerate emotional episodes with all their physiological, social and cognitive facets. The terminology of defense mechanisms comprises such terms as splitting-off, denial, dissociation and repression. With repressive inhibition, physiological and subjective components of emotional behavior will be repressed and cognitive aspects will be emphasized. Since physiological components are no longer integrated into behavior, the motivation for expressive-emotional behavior decreases as well. Unfortunate consequences of this repressive process are an extended activation of physiological, endocrine and immunological activation and a lack of coping. In stressful situations this leads to extended psycho-physiological reactions and ineffective coping (Schwarz & Kline 1995).

SUPPRESSIVE INHIBITION means that a person experiences emotional episodes completely and consciously but for some reason intentionally suppresses these episodes completely or partially. This suppression can be either arbitrary or conditioned by socialization. Resulting from suppression, physiological activation can occur which is similar to repressive inhibition, social regulation can be disturbed by lack of expressiveness and cognitive processing can be incomplete. The suppression of emotional experience can refer to different aspects of emotional behavior. The attempt to suppress cognitive components of emotional experience leads to an increased attention towards these split-off elements of emotional behavior which paradoxically results in an increased cognitive focus on suppressed contents. The processing of negative emotions will be impaired by suppressive inhibition, even if a person is conscious of this suppression, as potential coping behavior is missing. Gross & Levenson (1993) presented various silent film scenes to subjects (one neutral film scene with a park and two medical scenes with burnt skin and an amputation) and examined the effects of suppressive inhibition. From earlier attempts, the research team knew that both aversive film scenes were mainly judged to be disgusting and always provoked corresponding nonverbal behavior. Half the subjects were asked not to show their feelings. As could be expected, subjects who were given the »inhibition« instruction could control their facial expression. Somatic activity in the form of body movements and touching their face were significantly reduced. The deliberate suppression of emotional expression led to increased sympathetic arousal. Subjective disgust ratings were slightly reduced but ratings of anger, pain, grief, embarrassment and tension tended to increase. Contempt, a feeling that is expressively similar to disgust, was also significantly increased.

Deception, as a specimen of emotional inhibition, refers to when we are misinformed about another person's subjective emotional experience.

DECEPTIVE INHIBITION describes a strategy in dealing with emotions and usually refers to the communication of emotional content or to nonverbal behavior. Deceptive inhibition is usually incomplete but still requires a considerable amount of psychological power which can be manifested in vegetative arousal during deceptive attempts. Other consequences of deception are the incomplete processing of negative events and restricted social support which can be even more problematic. Buck (1984) differentiates three types of deception: non-emotional, stressful and emotional deception. Since deception without any emotional background can be neither recognized by behavior nor cause any physiological reactions, it is not of interest here. Rather it is not deception in general but stressful and emotional deception, which is of crucial interest. If deception is accompanied by conflict its behavioral manifestations can be easily recognized. People blink more often, delay an expected response, clear their throat more often, talk slower and have more speech impediments when they talk.

The Guilty Knowledge Test (GKT) is a laboratory model for stressful inhibition by deception. By using this method, an increased heart rate, breathing frequency and blood pressure could be shown for the moments of deception – these are all physiological reactions which are also known as a stress response. Video recordings which were made during the act of deception showed that inhibition not only leads to a physiological increase in arousal but also to a general inhibition of facial activity. For the duration of vegetative arousal the face seemed to freeze.

Pathways between stress, emotional inhibition and health disorders

Inhibition of emotions leads to disease via neurobiological, socio-behavioral and cognitive pathways. And even if the inhibition of emotional behavior does not cause disease, it can maintain disease or delay healing. Physiological over-arousal can have the same negative effect as an over-stimulated endocrine system or a dysregulated immune system. Healing is enhanced by caring treatment from the social environment. Inhibited emotional processing itself does not necessarily have to cause diseases but it can influence the course of diseases. The present model differentiates between health disorders and disease behavior. A detailed (and graphic) presentation of the pathway model can be found in Traue (1998). The following sections provide detailed descriptions of the three pathways from inhibition to disease.

Neurobiological pathways

There is no doubt that behavioral inhibition in little children in the presence of novel social stimuli, which is expressed in emotional inhibition, anxiety and shyness, has a neurobiological basis. Particularities of this behavioral pattern can be shown in low thresholds for new stimuli and in hyperactivity of certain physiological systems which is expressed as an increased fright reaction, increased muscle tension and for uninhibited children in overactive and easily excitable neurotransmitter systems.

A concept which is frequently discussed in this context assumes that the balance between activation and inhibition of neural activity favors inhibition.

Jeffrey Gray (1972, 1976) and Henri Laborit (1986, 1993) postulate a system of behavioral inhibition in the central nervous system. According to Gray, the behavioral inhibition system (BIS) reacts to unknown stimuli, pain stimuli and the frustrating absence of an expected response-contingent reward. Neuro-anatomically, the BIS is located in the septum-hippocampus-frontal (SHF) cortical region. Pharmacological substances such as barbiturates, alcohol and tranquilizers have a disinhibitory effect on the SHF region. Lesions in the SHF region also have a disinhibitory effect. The basic scheme of Gray's studies follows an experimental approach and avoidance conflict tested with animals. The experimental animals learn a certain behavior to get rewarded. When the reaction is learned, a punishing stimulus will be set that activates the BIS and reduces this learned behavior. This finally leads to a behavioral stop by passive avoidance with a simultaneous increase of neuro-physiological arousal and attention. The behavioral inhibition system reacts to conditioned punishing stimuli, stimuli which signal the end of a reward and to unknown stimuli. If then a fear-reducing substance is given which blocks the BIS, the effect of these stimuli will disappear and can be followed by approach behavior.

Based on his own studies and other scientific studies of unavoidable aversive stimuli, Henri Laborit (1986, 1993) developed a brain model of behavioral inhibition which is similar to Gray's and essentially refers to structures that enable the conditioning of fear stimuli. He considers behavioral inhibition itself to be a learned behavior. According to Laborit, the inhibition is transmitted via the ventral-median hypothalamus by releasing norepinephrine and ACTH. This is influenced by the dorsal septum region, the dorsal hippocampus and the lateral amygdala. The neurotransmitter serotonin (5-HT) increases the arousal of behavioral inhibition. Hereby, the dopaminergic system and acetylcholine influence the prefrontal cortex. According to Laborit, the serotonergic projections from the raphe nuclei into the neuronal system of septum, hippocampus and the prefrontal cortex as well as the cholinergic projections to the frontal cortex and the ascending pathways from the formatio reticularis and the basal nucleus of the amygdala are part of the behavioral inhibition system. The ascending cholinergic pathways to the cortex activate ACTH and the emission of cortisol. Henri Laborit describes the involvement of conditioned behavioral inhibition in the origin and maintenance of diseases as follows: » (1) Glucocorticoids lead to a blockage of the immune system. It can be deduced that if microbial infection or abnormal cells appear, which normally would be controlled by immune defenses, then an infectious or neoplastic episode may develop unhindered. This explains the relation between infections and neoplasms in behavioral situations where gratifying action is inhibited. It also shows that infectious agents or cancer-causing factors are not the only ones involved. (2) The peripheral release of norepinephrine at sympathetic system terminals will cause a generalized vasoconstriction, thus a decrease in the vascular container. Also, glucocorticoids lead to a retention of salts and water and so there is an increase in the vascular contents. The combination of these two facts leads to hypertension. Experimental observations also suggest that numerous somatic disturbances are generated by the same process: atherosclerosis, gastric ulcers, renal lesions, etc. (3) Concerning mental pathology, it is not in the scope of the present work to develop the consequences of inhibition of action. They may be summarized by saying that, in our opinion, anxiety and its neurotic consequences result from the conflict between the impulse to act and the inhibition of action, in this case from learning that punishment will follow the release of the impulse. Psychosis could be a flight into the imaginary when inhibition is too painful to be tolerated. (4) It is also interesting to note that in the scheme we have outlined, free radicals (H_2O_2, leukotrines, endoperoxides) are capable of destroying cellular membranes, those of lysosomes in particular, which may cause neural death. This could be a primary and fundamental step towards understanding the chronic state of certain diseases (Parkinson, Alzheimer), just as in acute lesions caused by cerebral anoxia.« (p. 73–74, 1993).

A clinical study can be cited to explain the relevance of Gray's and Laborit's postulated connections between behavioral inhibition and physiological and endocrine activations for the origin of a disease: In a study by Cole et al. (1996) with 222 HIV-seronegative, homosexual men as subjects, the negative effects of suppressing emotionally important sexual preferences could be demonstrated. By means of a secrecy scale the subjects were separated in four groups according to the degree of their outing: *completely out of the closet, mostly out of the closet, half in and half out of the closet und mostly or completely in the closet.* This also defines the degree to which homosexuals hide their sexual tendencies outside of their intimate area of life. The regression analysis resulted in a dramatic increase of disease frequency combined with an increased observance of secrecy for almost all infectious diseases as well as for skin cancer. Considering all diseases, the probability of disease doubles with each secrecy level. This effect has to be taken even more seriously since the effects of age, ethnicity, education, social status, health behavior (e.g. drug abuse, sleeping habits and physical fitness) and psychological influences such as depression, fear and negative affectivity – even repressive coping style – were eliminated from the data. Using a cross-sectional design such as this, this quasi-experimental study can not provide proof that inhibition leads to illness, and other causal directions are also possible (e.g. becoming sick could lead to less outing). However, all things considered, this study provides strong evidence that the degree of hiding sexual tendencies can be a releasing factor for disease.

Aside from the postulate of central nervous activity which can hinder emotional behavior, the hypothesis of conscious and unconscious processing of emotional information has been pursued since the beginning of the split-brain research. Former studies by Sperry (1966, 1974) describe the following: The right hemisphere processes graphic information (e.g. a naked woman in an experiment) into an appropriate emotional reaction (blushing, giggling), without knowing linguistically which information finally led to this emotional reaction. If we did not know that the transfer of information from the right to the left hemisphere was interrupted due to their separated corpus callosum, we would probably think of the defense mechanism of repression. It is well known that the female subject of this experiment does not intentionally suppress emotional content. Due to her neuropsychological deficit she is rather not able to describe it. Even if the results of split-brain human beings cannot be easily transferred to healthy people, these observations favor various ideas of a differentiated involvement of both hemispheres in the dysfunctional processing of emotional stimuli which is shown in inhibited expressiveness or alexithymia, since even with healthy human beings there are differences between the left and the right hemisphere in processing emotional information. This is of great importance for the issue of inhibited emotional expressiveness: With manual reaction the right hemisphere is faster than the left one in recognizing faces as carrying emotional information. But when reactions have to be linguistic, the right hemispheric advantage will disappear. Facial recognition tasks for physiognomic invariance (i.e. recognizing faces from different perspectives) are better solved by the right hemisphere. With the processing of acoustic stimuli the right hemisphere is dominant in identifying the emotional tone of language. From the difference in emotional processing within the left and right hemisphere, a neuropsychological mechanism can be derived which explains dissociations between emotional experience, emotional expressive behavior and physiological reactions that are typical for different phenomena of inhibited emotionality and personality (see Traue, 1988, 1998; Lane et al. 1995, 1996). An unpublished MRI study by Gündel et al. (unpublished) confirms the hypothesis that the volume of the right hemisphere correlates with the characteristic of alexithymia – but specifically only the anterior gyrus cinguli and only in male subjects.

Socio-behavioral pathways

Inhibited emotional processing means that people who cannot (appropriately) show their feelings in interpersonal situations have an essential deficit in communication, emotional exchange and relationships. As soon as a child is born, innate emotionality has an effect on the communicative behavior of parents. The more expressive a baby, the more parents address it using emotional facial expression. Emotional expressive reactions have an intensifying effect on both sides. The longing for emotional exchange always stays alive (Rimé 1995).

Children with lower expressiveness and increased sympathetic arousal are easier to condition since they react more strongly to punishing stimuli. Under unfavorable socialization conditions within the family, school or religious groups, growing emotional expressiveness can be suppressed and sympathetic arousal can be increased. There are other effects: Expressive children (and adults) are popular, seem to be more attractive and are superior in attaining their ends. Salovey and Mayer (1990) coined the term of »emotional intelligence« to describe this capability. When expressive persons use emotional intelligence, they succeed in building a social support system which, under stressful conditions, might serve as a buffer against stress and may reduce health-damaging effects.

Under extreme trauma emotional intelligence comes into play only if the person stays in his or her social environment and if they use their still existing emotional resources little by little to rebuild their social relationships (Traue et al. 1997; Traue 1998). Learning processes under extreme trauma can condition hyperactive arousal patterns in the autonomic nervous system – ranging from fear to external numbness and internal apathy. After having been conditioned, these human beings suffer from strong oscillations between high emotional arousal and emotional insensitivity, between the urge to run away and numbness.

Cognitive pathways

Memories of emotional experiences are often unpleasant, especially when they refer to problematic episodes in life. Therefore many human beings try to suppress thoughts of such events. Since such thoughts are crucial parts to emotional reactions, attempts to suppress them are inhibitions of emotional behavior. The energy used to suppress such thoughts is not available for use in other cognitive processes, resulting in reduced cognitive functioning.

The ambivalence with respect to emotional expressiveness can be interpreted as cognitive inhibition. King et al. (1992) formulated a theory of emotional ambivalence according to which the need for emotional expressiveness can cause conflicts which result in ambivalence with respect to one's own expressiveness. King's ambivalence questionnaire was translated into German and the connection between physical and psychological health and emotional ambivalence was tested on a sample of healthy test subjects. (Deighton & Traue, in preparation).

A factor analysis of the German AEQ resulted in two different ambivalence aspects regarding content. One factor summarized questions which referred to the consequences of emotional expressiveness, e.g. if someone fears that his expression of anger will be taken badly by another person. That is why we called this factor *effect ambivalence*. The second factor comprised questions which referred to one's ability to show an emotional expression, e.g. if someone wants to show his feelings but does not succeed. Therefore we call this factor *competence ambivalence*. Effect ambivalence mostly refers to negative emotions, whereas competence ambivalence is more connected with positive feelings. Both factors also differ in terms of health data. While effect ambivalence correlates with physical pain and depressive symptoms, high values in competence ambivalence correlate with a lack of social support.

Another cognitive pathway of suppression is caused by a cognitive style of processing emotional events lacking emotion . Many aspects have to be encoded linguistically in order to process an emotional event completely. Inner dialogues as well as the communication of emotional experiences require such linguistic transformations. Some decades ago scholars of psychosomatic medicine coined the term alexythymia for emotionless language to describe the incapability of dealing mentally or linguistically with emotional events. Maintaining a complete cognitive representation of emotional events is important in order to delete such events from the network of fear within the brain and to reconnect them to less frightening experiences. Due to the fact that in mental fear, networks of isolated emotional contents are associated with corresponding sympathetic arousal, physiological arousal could be interpreted as a physical symptom of disease.

Cognitive transformations of stressful events do not necessarily require the suppression of emotional information. One may capitalize on

Shakespeare's insight in Hamlet: »there is nothing either good or bad, but thinking makes it so.« and can try to change a certain way of feeling by changing one's way of thinking. Although reappraisal may include thought suppression, it mainly comprises reframing an emotional event in unemotional terms and the separation of internal states from external stimulation. In a recent study with functional magnetic resonance imaging, Ochsner et al. (2002) showed that the effective reduction of subjective negative affect by cognitive reappraisal correlates with increased activity in the left lateral, medial prefrontal and cingulate regions and decreased activation in the amygdala and medio-orbitofrontal cortex. Although these findings suggest that cognitive processes are involved in emotional regulation and can change subjective aversive experience, questions remain about the functional significance of this brain activity and their relevance for clinical populations. However, these observations are consistent with findings from treatment studies in depressive and obsessive-compulsive disorders, which found a normalization of prefrontal and amygdala activity. Therefore cingulate, prefrontal and amygdala activation seems to be relevant for emotional regulation.

Emotions in psychotherapy

Internal experience and expression of emotions are often the focus of attention in psychotherapy. Here, emotional behavior cannot be considered apart from cognitive processes and actions, since these functions can cause emotions and are also influenced by emotions. In the field of psychotherapy, which deals with the whole human being, emotional behavior can only be examined in connection with other basic psychological functions.

From a historical point of view, psychoanalysis used an energy term to describe emotional behavior since cybernetic concepts and ideas of processing information had not been developed at that time. In this context, Freud originally regarded emotional behavior in the sense of psychological energy, which had its origin in drives and instincts, the id. In the field of psychoanalysis the attention to emotional processes derived from clinical experiences with treating conditions formerly called hysteria. According to Freud, affects that are not abreacted stay mentally connected with the corresponding situation. Even if they remain unconscious, they can still cause neurotic behavior in which aspects of originally experienced or resulting motives are symbolized. Freud also took the view that an abreaction of experienced affect could either occur spontaneously during or following an affect-provoking situation or could result from a therapeutic intervention. Here, he had different possibilities in mind, which ranged from directly acting out one single event up to finely tuned talking about the trauma in several sessions (Freud, 1895).

Even if in traditional psychoanalysis the support of expressive emotionality had been forced back in favor of purely cognitive processes, these ideas were not lost. Michael Balint reported that Sandor Ferenczi experimented with so-called »active techniques«. Ferenczi assumed that in therapeutic sessions suppressed emotions, conflicts or thoughts can be stirred up in a way that they become almost conscious but due to their negative content are finally transformed into physical symptoms which can be understood and interpreted as neurotic symptoms.

Patients' physical behavior in therapy should be observed in regard to its expressive quality as the conflict between an emotional impulse to act and its suppression is reflected in physical-expressive behavior. Nowadays we talk about a different kind of nonverbal expressive behavior. Ferenczi regarded the liberation of the original impulse to act as an important step in therapy. In this context he suggested extending the passive analytical attitude by either recommending to patients that they actively live out their impulses or by advising them not to do so. From the present point of view it is amazing to see the amount of mental and intellectual effort analysts of the twenties took to find out whether they should advise patients to masturbate or not whenever they had that sexual impulse. However, outside the field of psychoanalysis it has been common practice to actively help patients to cope with their inhibited emotions, needs and impulses to act.

According to Ferenczi, his active technique considerably differed from the traditional method of free association. Ferenczi argued with his colleagues whether it was possible to hold a neutral position towards patients. He maintained that professional dishonesty might have the same damaging effect on patients as their original trauma (for Ferenczi's methods of treatment see Balint, 1967).

Two psychoanalysts must be mentioned when therapeutic concepts for the change of emotional inhibition are discussed: Carl G. Jung and

Wilhelm Reich. Both were psychoanalytic traditionalists but represented such radical views that new therapeutic schools derived from their work. Years before the already mentioned current discussion of emotion theory, Jung pointed out some essential differences between cognitive and emotional appraisals of environmental stimuli. According to him, cognitions lead to true-false-judgments whereas emotions lead to good-bad evaluations. Jung believed that both appraisal processes were rational, whereas in his opinion processes of perception and intuition were irrational and had to undergo rational evaluation by cognitions and emotions. All of these four psychological functions are important to behavior. In therapy underdeveloped psychological functions need to be supported. Another aspect of Jung's perspective regards the psyche as a self-regulating system. Suppressed memories and experiences become emotionally connected mental complexes within the unconscious and must be controlled by the individual. Rigid attitudes and behavioral rules adopted by the individual counteract these denied or suppressed mental complexes. In therapy the individual needs to experience these dreaded libidinal or destructive emotions in order to learn how to tolerate and accept them. It needs to be mentioned that Jung did not regard libido in a narrow sexual sense but as mental energy.

More radical and determined than any other psychoanalyst, Wilhelm Reich turned his back on a »purely intellectual understanding« of human emotions and on traditional psychoanalysis which in his opinion had made a mistake in giving up catharsis. He was interested in searching therapeutic possibilities for releasing suppressed emotions in therapy.

Wilhelm Reich assumed that any resistance to experience, to live and express feelings would be firmly embodied within the personality. Based on the psychological analysis of »character armoring«, as he called this resistance, he developed psycho- and physio-therapeutic interventions to break these armors. Basically he assumed that fear and fear of aggressiveness would cause the suppression of emotional impulses. Wilhelm Reich concentrated on physical symptoms and expressions in therapy more consistently than Ferenczi. He began to be more interested in nonverbal behavior than in verbal statements of his patients. He did not regard physical symptoms as transformed psychological energy but as manifestations of suppressed emotion.

According to Reich, muscular tensions did not result from the repression of feelings, but were the somatic mechanisms of the suppression of feelings themselves. His therapy aimed at breaking muscular armor, revealing suppressed emotional impulses and developing an awareness of situations in which the suppression of emotions had originated.

Wilhelm Reich did not value the concept of catharsis for its own sake. This was often misunderstood. He believed that catharsis helped to release emotions and make patients aware of them. Emotions should not be released and expelled from internal psychic processes, but should rather be consciously perceived and accepted. Cathartic elements in therapy were followed by a phase of mental processing of experienced feelings. Suppression was counteracted by realization and clarification of the involved psychological mechanisms. Wilhelm Reich worked with a mixture of breathing techniques, massage and physical exercises which increased the general level of arousal to a point at which finally the resistance to suppressed feelings could be given up. In Reich's therapy this support of emotional expressiveness was the ideal way to physical and mental health.

Emotional behavior plays an important role in body-oriented forms of psychotherapy. Strongly influenced by Reich's ideas of emotional inhibition and his therapeutic techniques, Alexander Lowen developed Bioenergetic Analysis – a therapeutic school that considers physical and intensive emotional experience to be the central elements of healing. In line with Wilhelm Reich, Alexander Lowen assumes that emotional inhibition absorbs psychic energy which would be necessary for an individual's active coping with his environment. Similar to C.G. Jung, he emphasizes the function of emotional stimuli for the interpretation of internal and external stimuli: Knowledge associated with feelings becomes understanding and can induce change (Lowen, 1975, S. 62).

According to Alexander Lowen, expressive emotionality leads to an improved coordination of psychic and somatic processes and integrates thoughts and attitudes. Bioenergetic theory considers emotional expressiveness to be healthy because of its regulating effects on the social environment as well as on the personal self. Physical movements and changes in posture support the expression of strong emotions.

Lowen considers both neurotic and psychosomatic disorders to be caused by traumatic experiences or emotional deprivation in childhood.

It is possible to react both with inhibition of emotions and impulsivity. Lowen was convinced that parents instill the suppression of feelings into their children because they have low tolerance for their and other children's emotional expression. LikeWilhelm Reich, Lowen considered the abreaction of and liberation from trauma, mainly experienced in childhood, to be the crux of therapy.

In response to the results of research in childhood development and emotion theory, finally even in the field of psychoanalysis it has become generally accepted that emotional behavior has to be understood as a communication system by means of which needs, wishes and situational appraisals can be more directly communicated into the social environment nonverbally than verbally.

Current psychotherapeutic theories almost unanimously hold the experience and expression of emotions as very important for understanding patients and their disorders. Emotional behavior in therapy is often regarded as the key to change: Greenberg and Safran describe this change in the following episode:

> »I saw a therapist for a few months and began to talk about some of my feelings of isolation and frustration. The issues became somewhat more crystallized for me, but, somehow or other, things didn't really change for me on an emotional level. Then I began to see a second therapist. Somehow or other, this therapist began to get me in touch with what I was feeling inside. I remember, much to my surprise, breaking down and crying in the second session. I began by making weak sounds and soon was wailing and crying at the top of my lungs. Gradually, over the next five minutes, the intensity of my crying subsided. I began to talk about the pain and desperation I was experiencing inside in a way I never had before. Perhaps I had never felt it that way before, either. I continued talking about my sense of longing for human contact, and the way I felt caged in by my anxieties and fears of rejection, my guilt feelings about having a sexual relationship. In the following weeks I began to feel more and more motivated to do things to change my life. It was a few months before I made big changes on the outside, but I'll always date the beginning of the change back to that episode« (Greenberg & Safran 1987, S. 4).

Patients start to react emotionally at a certain point in the therapeutic process. This emotional moment differs from former feelings in its intensity and its expressive component. Patients really feel themselves and thus obtain insight. Due to this intense feeling they are able to talk more clearly about their needs and to develop motives. The crucial emotional processes are subjective experiences of feelings, physical involvement, emotional expression as well as resultant motivational and cognitive changes. Many psychotherapists would agree on the fact that psychological problems often result from the blocking or avoidance of potentially adaptive emotional behavior and that psychotherapeutic interventions aim at overcoming the resistance to emotions and at revealing emotional experience, and that furthermore the complete living out of a specific emotional episode leads to a change of emotional experience and thus enables new adaptive reactions in problematic situations.

If we would like to analyze how the science of psychotherapy deals with patients' emotional processes, one cannot really talk about »psychotherapy« since in numerous psychotherapeutic traditions the theory which they are based on differs considerably from their therapeutic interventions. In theory differences between schools are bigger than in therapeutic practice.

Four dimensions of emotion therapy

Greenberg & Safran (1987) postulated four essential dimensions. These are based on different psychotherapeutic perspectives from which emotional behavior is viewed within the corresponding therapeutic concepts and techniques of treatment:

1) Emotional discharge
2) Emotional insight
3) Facilitating adaptive emotions
4) Exposure and habituation

Different psychotherapeutic perspectives evaluate these four dimensions in different ways. But if one aspect (or more) is used within a psychotherapeutic intervention, it will be crucial to aim at a complete living out of an emotional episode including subjective experience, emotional expressiveness, physiological arousal and interactive functions.

Emotional Discharge: Many psychotherapeutic methods contain elements of catharsis more or less explicitly. Mostly cathartic elements are considered, e.g., to help to activate repressed memories or to offer patients a safe room where they do not have to flee from suppressed or avoided emotional reactions. Only a few therapists believe in the salutary effects of directly living out emotions such as the adherents of primal therapy. Even Thomas (1983), being an advocate of cathartic therapy, believes that catharsis is particularly effective if patients can observe their expression of previously repressed or suppressed emotions from a certain distance and if they can step by step remove their emotional inhibition by means of this self-experience and self-observation. The release of suppressed emotionality should be embedded in therapeutic strategies which strive for changes in a patient's self-concept after having had a cathartic experience, so that lasting changes can derive from cathartic experience. If assumptions concerning stress and coping were prominent in therapy, one aim of emotional discharge would be to direct the psychological effort necessary for suppressing emotions towards coping with stress. This aim can only be achieved if patients previously acknowledged the possibility and power of emotional discharge.

Emotional Insight: Although in psychotherapies which are largely cognitively oriented catharsis of emotional arousal is considered to be ineffective or at best to have ephemeral effects, the significance of emotional experiencing is not questioned. On the contrary: Purely intellectual understanding of one's own behavior – even of disturbed behavior – is to be distinguished from insight. Insight in therapy only occurs when emotional aspects of experience are processed concommitantly with remembered events. Insight is only effective if patients understand their emotional impulses in the overall context of their personal and cultural value system and integrate the episode into a personal narrative. In psychoanalysis, for example, the rendering process serves the goal of emotionally enriching previously superficial, psychological experiences via the mechanism of transference. The closer current emotional experience and intellectual processing are related to each other, the more likely patients are to change. In client-centered therapy therapists specifically focus on emotional nuances in their patients' verbal communications. Client-centered therapy deals not so much with suppressed emotional impulses but rather with emotionally communicated aspects patients' self-concepts and relationships to social objects of their interpersonal environment. Here, emotions are regarded as meaningful processes by means of which an individual evaluates its inner and outer world. In this respect, insight is always connected with emotional involvement. Among other forms of therapy, client-centered therapy explicitly focuses on the opposite process, on the constructivist perspective of experienced emotionality. Any personal self-concept is always the result of a mental construction and can only be complete if it includes emotional experience. In this respect, subjective and present emotional experience are necessary to change self-concepts in therapy.

FACILITATING ADAPTIVE EMOTIONS: By facilitating adaptive emotions, the self-centered individual perspective is extended. For an individual within his social context, emotions control his behavior and experience within interpersonal contact. Sympathy, attraction and the rejection of other persons are regulated by emotional experience. In this context the role of emotions as a system of processing information according to an intra- and inter-individual dimension is emphasized. It opens the view beyond the individual. Therapeutic methods which restrict their striving to a reduction of unwanted feelings, neglect and ignore the adaptive value of emotional reactions.

The communicative meaning of expressive emotional behavior is at the core of humanistic therapy. Expressive emotional behavior is supported, thereby enabling patients to translate their subjective spectrum of feelings into interpersonal communication. The same applies to social competence training in behavior therapy where expressive emotional behavior is practiced or supported in order to fulfill needs or solve problems.

Present development of different therapeutic concepts is characterized by an effort to integrate new findings from psychobiology. This applies to cognitive-behavioral therapies which help traumatized patients to cope with the neurobiological effects of extreme stress on emotional behavior as well as to the field of psychoanalysis which nowadays integrates findings from developmental psychology into its own concepts. Expressive emotional behavior probably developed phylogenetically from general behavior patterns (e.g. vomiting rejected food) to the communication of appraisals (e.g. disgust). Hence, the adaptive function of expressive behavior for living in groups must be high.

EXPOSURE AND HABITUATION: Methods of catharsis, flooding or implosion are based on different theoretical ideas. They also have their roots in different therapeutic approaches (early psychoanalysis and behavioral therapy). Their theoretical background assumes that potentially existing emotional behavior might disturb patients if it is triggered by certain stimuli or if it is unwanted. Early psychoanalysts viewed these unwanted reactions as well as their qualitative transformations via abreaction in catharsis, so-to-say as creating a valve for discharging psychic energy. Behavior therapists thought that extinction and counter-conditioning would be an appropriate means of therapy, either by conditioning an alternative reaction to situations which previously caused unwanted feelings or by revoking consequences which increased unwanted feelings. Emotional behavior has to occur during therapeutic sessions, i.e. it has to be introduced by an active process, to make therapeutic strategies successful. This is an essential common feature. In recent behavioral-therapeutic discussions, the term of *emotional processing* is used. Emotional processing reflects the transition of therapeutic goals from reducing unwanted emotions to behavioral alternatives. Stanley Rachman says: »As a start, emotional processing is regarded as a process whereby emotional disturbances are absorbed, and diminish to the extent that other experiences and behaviour can proceed without disruption.« (Rachman 1980, 51). All of these therapeutic methods use different techniques from different psychotherapeutic schools but have in common that they seek to promote emotional processing or the understanding of one's emotions.

Conclusion

The described model of health and illness postulating a connection between inhibited emotionality and disorders of health is a non-deterministic pathway model which describes neurobiological, socio-behavioral and cognitive pathways between stress and emotional activation, their processing by inhibition and clinical consequences. In particular for headaches and back-pain, diseases of the cardiovascular system and cancer, there are numerous empirical and partly even experimental results which prove beyond theoretical assumptions the clinical relevance of inhibited emotionality as a risk factor to health. Contemporary psychotherapists and scholars of psychosomatic medicine are not alone having discovered the damaging effects of emotional inhibition to physical health. In various civilizations, the individual costs for the inhibition of individual emotions which are based on social constraints – and good reasons – were and are at least partly reduced by rituals of emotional openness. Rituals of emotional openness in ethnic groups and former historical epochs are nowadays removed from their mostly religious context by modern psychotherapy and experience a secularized form of professionalism as well as a wide proliferation of psychological concepts into everyday life.

Psychological therapy processes which are well-known in the field of psychosomatic and behavioral medicine aim almost unanimously at changing emotional behavior in order to reduce physical stress reactions. In conclusion it must be said that in the field of psychotherapy, emotion-regulating interventions have proven to be very successful with the treatment of emotional problems and inhibition and with disorders of physical health (Traue, 1998).

References

Alexander, F. (1950): Psychosomatic Medicine. New York (Norton).

Balint, M. (1967): Sandor Ferenczi's Technical Experiments. In Benjamin B. Wolman (Ed.) Psychoanalytic Techniques, New York (Basic Books).

Buck, R. (1984): The communication of Emotion. New York (Guilford Press).

Chorover, S. L. (1979): From genesis to Genocide. The Meaning of Human Nature and the Power of Behavioral Control. NewYork (Bantam Books)

Cole, S. W., M. E. Kemmeny, S. E. Taylor & B. R. Visscher (1996): Elevated physical health risk among gay men who conceal their homosexual identity. Health Psychology 15(4), 243–251.

Damasio, A.R. (1994): Descartes' Error. Emotion, Reason and the Human Brain. New York (G. P. Putnam's Son).

Deighton, R.M. & Traue, H.C, (in preparation): Emotionale Ambivalenz: Zusammenhänge zu Körpersymptomen, Depressivität, und sozialer Interaktion. Drei Studien mit dem AEQ-G18

Elias, N. (1936): Über den Prozeß der Zivilisation. Frankfurt a.M. (Suhrkamp).

Erk, S. & Walter, H. (2000): Denken mit Gefühl. Nervenheilkunde 19, 3–13.

Field, T.M., Woodson, R., Greenberg, R, & Cohen, D. (1982): Discrimination and imitation of facial expressions in neonates. Science, 218, 179–181.

Dunbar, H.F. (1935): Emotions and bodily changes: A survey of the literature: 1919–1933. New York (Columbia University Press).

Freud, S. (1904/1905, 1942): Bruchstücke einer Hysterie-Analyse. Gesammelte Werke, London (Imago, Band V, S. 240).

Freud, S. (1895): Entwurf einer Psychologie. In: Aus den Anfängen der Psychoanalyse. Frankfurt (Fischer Verlag (1975)).

Gray, J. A. (1972). The psychophysiological nature of introversion – extraversion: A modification of Eysenck's theory. In: Nebylitsyn, V.D. & Gray, J.A. (Hrsg.) Biological basis of individual behavior. New York: Academic Press.

Gray, J.A. (1976):The behavioral inhibition system: A possible substrate for anxiety. In: M. P. Feldmann & A. M. Broodhurst (Hrsg.). Theoretical and experimental base of behavior modification. New York (John Wiley & Sons).

Greenberg, L. S. & J. D. Safran (1987): Emotion in Psychotherapy. New York (The Guilford Press).

Gross, J. J. & R. W. Levenson (1993): Emotional suppression: Physiology, self-report and expressive behavior. Journal of Personality and Social Psychology 64, 970–986.

Gündel, A., A.O. Ceballos-Baumann, A. López, J. Deus, N. Cardoner, B. Marten-Mittag, M. von Rad und J.Pujol (unpublished): Alexithymia correlates with the size of the right anterior cingulate gyrus.

Hochschild, A.R. (1983): The Managed Heart. Commercialisation of Human Feelings. Berkley/Los Angeles (The University of Calofornia Press).

Heller, B. W. (1983): Emotion: T-oward a biopsychosocial paradigm. In: L. Temoshok, C. van Dyke & L. S. Zegans (eds.) Emotions in Health and Illness. New York (Grune & Stratton, 190–194).

James, William (1890): The principles of psychology. New York (Holt).

Kagan, J., J. S. Reznick & N. Snidman (1988): Biological bases of childhood shyness. Science 240(4849), 167–71.

King, L. A., R. A. Emmons & S. Woodley (1992): The structure of inhibition. Journal of Research in Personality 26, 85–102.

Laborit, H. (1986): L'inhibition d'action. Paris (Masson (2. Ed.)).

Laborit, H. (1993): Inhibition of action: interdisciplinary approach to its mechanism and physiopathology. In: H. C. Traue & J. W. Pennebaker (Hrsg.): Emotion, Inhibition, and Health. Seattle (Hogrefe & Huber Publishers, 57–80).

Lane , R. D., L. S. Kiveley, M. A. du Bois, P. Shamasundara & G. E. Schwartz (1995): Levels of emotional awareness and the degree of right hemispheric dominance in the perception of facial emotion. Neuropsychologia, 33, 525–538.

Lane, R. D., L. Sechrest, R. Reidel, V. Weldon, A. Kasznlak & G. E. Schwartz (1996): Impaired verbal and nonverbal emotion recognition in alexithymia. Psychosomatic Medicine, 58, 203–210.

Lowen, A. (1975): Pleasure: A creative approach. Baltimore (Penguin Books).

Mills, C. W. (1956): White Collar. New York (Holt).

Ochsner, K.N., Bunge, S.A., Gross, J.J. and Gabrieli, J.D.E. (2002): Rethinking Feelings: An fMRI Study of the Cognitive Regulation of Emotion. Journal of Cognitive Neuroscience 14:8, pp. 1215–1229

Pennebaker, J. W. (1995): Emotion, disclosure, & health: An overview. In J. W. Pennebaker (ed.): Emotion, disclosure, and health. Washington, D. C. (American Psychological Association, 3–10).

Rachman, S. (1980): Emotional Processing. Behavior Research and Therapy 18, 51–60.

Reich, W. (1933, Edition 1973): Die Charakteranalyse, Frankfurt a.M. (Fischer Verlag).

Rimé, B. (1995): Mental Rumination, Social Sharing, and the Recovery from Emotional Exposure. In: J. W. Pennebaker (ed.): Emotion, disclosure, and health. Washington, D. C. (American Psychological Association, 271–292).

Salovey, P. & J. D. Mayer (1990): Emotional Intelligence. Imagination, Cognition, and Personality 9, 185–211.

Schwartz, G. E., & Kline, J. P. (1995): Repression, Emotional Disclosure and Health. In J. W. Pennebaker (Ed.): Emotion, disclosure, and health. Washington, D.C. (American Psychological Association)

Sherrington, C. S. (1932): Inhibition as a coordinative factor. In: Nobel Foundation (Hg.): Nobel Lectures (Physiology and Medicine 1922–1941), 278–289.

Smith, R. (1992): Inhibition: History and meaning in the sciences of mind and brain. Berkeley, Los Angeles (University of California Press).

Sperry, R. W. (1966): Brain bisection and consciousness. In: J. Eccles (Hrsg.): Brain and conscious experience. New York (Springer).

Sperry, R. W. (1974): Lateral specialization in the surgicaby seperated hemispheres. In: F.O. Schmitt & F.G. Warden (Hrsg.): The Neurosciences Third Study Program. Cambridge, Mass. (MIT Press).

Traue, H.C. (1988): Cerebrale Lateralität, emotionale Prozesse und Krankheit. In W. Ehlers, H.C. Traue und D. Czogalik (Hrsg.): Bio-psycho-soziale Grundlagen für die Medizin. Heidelberg (Springer).

Traue, H. C. (1998): Emotion und Gesundheit. Die psychobiologische Regulation durch Hemmungen. Heidelberg (Spektrum).

Traue, H.C. (1999): Emotion. In: U. Tewes & K. Wildgrube (Hg.): Psychologie-Lexikon. München (Oldenbourg, 93–97).

Traue, H. C. & R. M. Deighton (2000): Emotional Inhibition. In: G. Fink (ed.): Encyclopedia of Stress. San Diego (Academic Press, Vol. 2, 32–38).

Traue, H. C. (2001): Emotional Inhibition and Health. In N. J. Smelser & P. B. Baltes (Eds.): The international encyclopedia of the social and behavioral sciences (Vol. 7, pp. 4449–54). Oxford, England (Elsevier).

Traue, H. C., M. Kessler & V. Lee (1997): Pathways linking emotional inhibition, psychosomatic disorders and pain. In: Ad Vingerhoets, F.v. Bussel & J. Boelhouwer (eds.): The (Non) Expression of Emotion in Health and Disease. Tilburg (Tilburg University Press, 193–210).

Traue, H. C. & J. W. Pennebaker (eds.) (1993): Emotion, Inhibition and Health. Toronto (Hogrefe & Huber Publishers).

Vingerhoets, Ad, F.v. Bussel & J. Boelhouwer (eds.) (1997): The (Non) Expression of Emotion in Health and Disease. Tilburg (Tilburg University Press).

Wouters, C. (1986): Formalization and informalization, changing tension balances in civilizing process. Theory, Culture and Society 3, 1–19.

A key note with this topic was given by Harald C. Traue at the annual conference of the IIBA 2003 in Salvador de Bahia in Brazil. It is based on a shortened, partly amended and translated version of Traue, H.C. and Deighton, R.M. (2003) Emotionale Hemmung als Risikofaktor für die Gesundheit. In: A. Stephan and H. Walter (Hrsg.) Natur und Theorie der Emotionen. Paderborn: Mentis Verlag.

Prof.Dr. Harald Traue, Health Psychology,
Dept. of Psychosomatic Medicine and Psychotherapy,
University of Ulm, Am Hochsträss 8, FRG,
e-mail: harald.traue@medizin.uni-ulm.de

The Space of Silence

Maê Nascimento

Introduction

Today Bioenergetic Analysis, and psychotherapy in general, must be evaluated within a larger context of our professional history, new findings, and our understanding of knowledge itself. In this short paper, I want to introduce what I consider to be an essential ingredient to such evaluation and to therapy itself – the space of silence. This is an inner place which the therapist consciously accesses, in order to reduce the continuous interference from the Ego and to become available to issues and information coming up in the therapist-client relationship.

To get there, I paint a very large canvas about knowledge and psychotherapy. I ask what we can learn from new concepts of the Self, from developments in neurobiological research and Physics. I ask what these insights portend for our perspective on health, disease and cure. This then leads to a consideration of new roles for the therapist. For simplicity's sake, I use the feminine pronoun in referring to the person.

The human being in modern psychology

Psychoanalysis was the first scientific theory to describe psychic functioning, how disturbances in this functioning contributed to disease and to provide a method for achieving psychological health. Sigmund Freud's insight into the intrinsic connection between Biology and Psychology was revolutionary. For this, he has been considered as the father of psychosomatic medicine. According to Freud's perspective, *sexuality* is the central focus in the human psyche and his views about pathology include a somatic basis for symptoms.

He created his theory in morally restrictive times, and his concepts and methods were cloaked in an atmosphere of secrecy. I have always pictured in my mind that when Freud's clients spoke up their associations, they might sound like whispering secrets, so ›prohibited‹ were Freud's discoveries regarding sexuality.

Repressed material (which Freud always interpreted as sexual) had to do with a natural vitality that could not be experienced and expressed – let alone valued. Freud's boldness in bringing sexuality to light was only partially successful. The sexual (thus biological) nature of psychic functioning/mal-functioning was described and analyzed only from a mental perspective.

It was Wilhelm Reich who formed the vanguard of a new position, proposing that pleasure and vitality could free human beings, allowing them to have a wider range of expression. With his *Functional identity* concept,[1] he joined the biological (the body) and the psyche into a totality through which the individual can be seen and through which the individual expresses herself in life. He also created the concept of the orgone, the universal vital energy in human beings and the cosmos.

Nevertheless, repressive forces of Fascism and Nazism rose to a peak at that time, which produced a ›disconnected mind‹ of submission. This repressive process eventually produced many revolutionary movements, claiming new values and ways of being. These movements appeared everywhere, perhaps with an apogee in the sixties with the multitude of movements around expression, of recovering senses and sensuality, giving room for the body as a focus. Those movements also emphasized love and peace, sexual freedom, community, gender equality and the like. New values were expressed by the Hippies, the Women's Liberation Movement, ecological awareness, anti-war sentiment, etc. They spoke of a new human being, more integrated and loving, throwing off the shibboleths of the past.

Psychology also reflected these times with new approaches to old problems – Psychodrama, Gestalt, Client Centered Therapy, Transactional Analysis and Bioenergetic Analysis. These psychotherapies brought in the scope of their theories an integration of sensation, feeling and thinking, and were humanistic in orientation. Everything seemed new and people

1 »The concept of Functional Identity ... only means that muscular attitudes and character attitudes have the same function in the psychic mechanism: they can replace each other and influence one another. They, basically, can not be apart. They are equivalent in their roles« (Reich 1977, p. 230).

were starting a wider and popular learning about themselves in the quest for ›authenticity‹ in living.

The context of psychotherapy

Daniel Goleman writes: »Psychology theories are shaped by self-biography: The author's personal history has direct influence over their theoretical constructions« (Goleman 1980, p. 33). Perhaps this helps to explain the reason why certain personal characteristics are learned as required attributes to the role of therapists or in their methods. Take Freud and Reich, for example: These new psychotherapeutic theoreticians were strong, determined and assertive men who totally believed in their ideas and concepts. Because they were bringing very new insights about the person, they faced opponents and resistance, but fought fiercely to have their approach and methods understood and they did so in a consistent and vigorous way. I think we can ›see‹ this vigor and firmness in their descriptions of therapeutic techniques, leading to the impression that those traits should be part of ›being a therapist‹.

Bioenergetics was also innovative in its time, with its conceptualization about energy and its view of the body. Such innovation might have motivated close surveillance as part of its teaching. This could be one reason for Alexander Lowen's and John Pierrakos' firm and personal attitudes being taken as part of the required attitude developed by many Bioenergetic therapists. At some point, it has been yet considered as a ›directive‹ psychotherapy approach, with the therapist looking at the client's body, making a diagnosis assessing the issue and suggesting ›exercises‹ to the client. The client is supposed to trust the therapist and follow his instructions. Perhaps also in those opening and changing times people needed parameters for the new ways of thinking and behaving. Thus strong and authoritarian leaders who model ›assertive‹ techniques would provide their clients and students with a feeling of being safe and protected in tracing a new path.

Some decades later, however, the scenery has changed – and perhaps therapeutic needs as well. The present time demands decreasing interference coming from the world over the person, a ceasing of the excessive demands of the past.

People, now, would rather seek inside themselves for dealing with issues which, in the past, were posed to parental figures from outside – such as the therapist.

A perspective based on today's knowledge

At this moment in time we are in transition to a new paradigm. Before introducing it, though, we should look at the process of knowledge itself. Throughout history, mankind has been going through an evolutionary path which is continuously changing.

»Development trajectories unfold in a spiral movement in both, individual and collective instances. Our existence follows an evolutionary pattern, going from simpler to more complex levels« (Basso & Pustilnik 2000, p. 18). This statement is yet supported by Psychology researchers in the field of child development.

Paradigms are organizing structures to aid us in our process of learning about the Universe. When formed, they give a new way of seeing the world and at a certain point they are discarded when new ones are formed. But when a paradigm is discarded, the knowledge it provided does not ›die‹ – it is transformed and incorporated into a new one.

Physics exemplifies this perhaps better than any other discipline. Until the middle of the 20th Century we lived in a Newtonian/Cartesian world, a world which was described as being solid, predictable and governed by defined rules. The mode of thinking and understanding was largely deductive and linear. Reality concepts were demonstrated by mathematical equations.

With the advent of Quantum and Chaos theories this world was turned upside down and the deterministic views of the past were questioned. From Physics we learn that atomic particles are neither solid nor predictable. They just *Potentially exist* (existing within certain probabilities). »Quantum Physics provides us with supportive data for intuitive phenomena which were implicit in all fields (mainly in Human Sciences) but could not be given a scientific status, since . . . they do not produce absolute mathematical equations« (Basso & Pustilnik 2000, p. 58). From these points of view, two inferences arise, both crucially important to the approach of the knowledge process:

Today's concepts of the Universe suggest mutant and unpredictable matter, which does not necessarily exist at defined places, but has a probability, a tendency of occurring.

A phenomenon can not be separated from its observer, the one who ›shapes‹ it in a certain time and place.

Those new concepts may suggest to us the idea of reality as being *conscience* which is expressed in the individualized (each one of us) consciousness and in mankind's collective consciousness.

This new perspective widens Psychology's scope and many of its key concepts, like *health, disease* and *cure*, may need to be reformulated or changed.

In Freud's theory, the concept of *health* is associated to the degree of Ego's development along the infantile period. There are many complex variables in this process: But to put it in a simple way, the Ego is the mediator between the person and the environment. It is the Ego then which sets the degree of adjustment or deviation from moral/ ethical/ behavioral codes. Reich's theory as well as Bioenergetics, have demonstrated the functional role of the Ego in the concept of character: Ego builds up a personality based on defensive mechanisms enhancing the person's being in the world in a more or less acceptable and ›painless‹ condition.

Ego, thus, has to do with social image, with what is expected from each person considering environmental conditions. Ego results from conditioning processes.

But we shall claim that the person is much more than her ›learned reactions‹ and probably for this reason, the concept of *self* has been receiving more and more focus.

Supportive concepts from the neurosciences

»The *self* can be seen as an integrative principle, operating at each and every level of development . . . As an organizing entity, it guides evolution through wholeness, and its perception can be a source of inspiration and healing« (Basso & Pustilnik 2000, p. 60). The issue of the Self being an individualized particle coming from the Universe totality cannot be seen as matters exclusive to Philosophy or Religion like they were in the past.

As I said, the new metaphor refers to a concept of reality which does not exist as fixed and settled independently of our attention. Instead, we deal with a *potential reality* being shaped according to our attention and perception of it. This perspective is supported by research in the *neurosciences*. I will report on these findings, in order to aid us in our comprehension of it.

Prior to the sixties/seventies, knowledge of the critical importance of the Central Nervous System was limited. It was seen as an electrical communication system where nervous transmissions occurred exclusively through *synapses* – electrical impulses going from one neuron to another, like walking ›step by step‹. The electrical brain was considered as the only one in charge of intellect and consciousness. If this was the correct description of its real nature, we would have pre-determined restrictions on our capacity to learn, according to the number of nervous terminations existing in our brain. In the late seventies, though, there was a radical change and new findings pointed to the existence of chemical substances and processes in the brain. These were referred to as *transmitters* and *receptors* and comprised the real information network.

According to Candace Pert (1999, p. 66), »We call *transmitters* any component, either natural or synthetic, which makes a connection to its specific *receptor* molecule in the cell's surface ... This transmitter, colliding and entwining [to the receptor] is what we call *liaison* (to connect) and in this process, it carries on the message – through molecular qualities, into the receptor (...) Receptors are molecules composed by proteins and they gather in a bunch in the cellular membrane, waiting for the right chemical ›keys‹ which will come ›swimming‹ through the extra-cellular fluids to meet them and to connect to them. These are the transmitters moving throughout the body, and when meeting their receptors, they connect and disconnect as in a network, in a simultaneous way, carrying information. The receptors work, basically, as sensing and sensorial molecules ... they work as sensorial organs, just at the cellular level. They flow over the membrane of cells ... *dancing* and *vibrating*, waiting to get the messages from other vibrating particles [the transmitters] which come across the cells. They are in continuous movement, *in a rythmic and vibratory way*... The connecting process is very selective, since receptors simply ignore all transmitters that are not meant to match or entwine with them«. This is a fascinating description of the information network, which works all through the body, providing a biochemical foundation for emotions.

In the Eighties transmitters and receptors have come to be known as *information molecules*, producing a cell's *language system* for communication among endocrine, gastric, neurological and immunological systems. We see, then, that the information system of the ›biochemical brain‹ works in accordance with the notion of totality and integration. Moreover, with information being an essential part of the process, we might assume that there is *intelligence* shaping systems and creating behaviors – not casual, random or intellectual, but an intelligence which is organizing, harmonizing and provides meaning. This intelligence is not an exclusive human quality, it comes from the Universe. As I see it, it does not work in deterministic ways, but as a tendency to integration and harmony.

New frame – new human being

Many authors have been referring to the concept of *self*, but with many different meanings. The *self* referred to in this paper is the same as used in Analytical Psychology and in Transpersonal Psychology: Its main idea has to do with the idea of totality.

»A human being is one part in a whole which we call ›Universe‹ – a part which is restricted to a certain time and space. She experiences herself, her thoughts and emotions as being separated from the whole – as in an optical illusion of the consciousness« (Einstein 1985, p. 13)

We are, then, a part within the wholeness of the ›Universe‹. From this perspective, each human being can experience herself as an Independent Self in her searching for wholeness. The Self encompasses everything a person is, even potentially and is far beyond what she learns throughout her life-span. The Self can be seen as possessing an endless source of qualities which, under appropriate conditions, can be revealed. Carl G. Jung wrote that »nobody understands what the Self is, because the Self is everything you are not – it is not the ego. The ego finds itself as an appendix of the Self« (Jung 1971, p. 31). In a similar statement, John Pierrakos describes the CORE as »... the centre of the individualized life ... it is the whole human capacity, a vital and luminous mass, the source and the conscience of the Vital Force« (Pierrakos 1990, p. 27). Considering that these concepts convey the qualities of wholeness and the possibility of human potential to be developed by each living person, we are reasoning here in accordance with the new paradigms.

New parameters for *health, disease* and *cure*

Health denotes integration. »Perfect mental health is fully connected to all other components of well-being. Wholeness, thus, depends on a balanced integration among the physical, mental, emotional, existential and spiritual levels of consciousness« (Vaughn 1980, p. 20). We live in a world with increasing levels of agitation and noise, and people, at least in Western cultures, try to adjust to this condition. As a consequence, the focus is kept outside the Self often with a frantic search for status and power, ›success‹ and wealth. This condition leads to psychic numbing, fragmentation, and to a progressive *loss of connection* to the Self, to the truest and deepest being inside us. It also means identification with the Ego as Self. This can be considered as a new framing of *disease* or *dysfunction*.

The person who has the Ego as a guide for her thoughts and behaviors restrains her potentiality to be in accordance with ›approved‹ emotions, feelings and thoughts. She also represses or denies healthy qualities resulting in conflicts and suffering. This process works on the vital energy flow by blocking and freezing and denying authenticity. As posed by Reich and Bioenergetics, the energy flow becomes fragmented, bringing distortions to the whole natural balance of the organism. Blocked energy reduces self-awareness and prevents consciousness from expanding through experience. The person stands stuck, devitalized and unable to feel herself into the experience of growing. As John Pierrokos points out:

> »From the perspective of our essential being, dysfunction comes about from unnatural flow of energy inside the organism . Dysfunctions are, then, expressed through denial patterns, which have common characteristics, but show unique combination in each individual« (Pierrakos 1990, p. 84).

Healing, then, has to do with dis-identifying Self from Ego and restoring connection to the vital energy flow which forms the Self. Free energy flowing represents the possibility, for all of us, of full realization of who we truly are, and this is provided by Self connection through consciousness. This quality restores to the person the condition of Wholeness – within herself and with the Universe.

A new therapeutic process

The process of dis-identification from the Ego and re-connection to the Self is very complex and not in the scope of this paper. However, I want to point out that this transformation requires the therapist to change his *internal attitude*. This change will reflect on his way of relating to the client. As I mentioned before, the healing process refers to mobilizing blocked energy altogether with its respective psychic contents. I refer here to what we know as character issues, which need to be worked through to allow awareness and integration. This condition gives Bioenergetics a privileged position as its main focus tends to be the energy in the body and its correspondent personal expressions. Yet, the Bioenergetic therapist must also be acutely aware of certain conditions in the therapeutic relationship which are related to her new internal attitude.

First of all – and this turns out to be a major transformation for those therapists who see their role as directive – directions do not come from a mental / Ego place. They come through the energy flow in the body, which, when it is allowed, will find its proper way. In order to apprehend those directions, the therapist must be in a *listening / observing*, rather than ›processing‹, mode. To be truly in that place, the therapist must shut up his own Ego chitchat, stopping its continuous judgmental interference. She needs to be in contact with her own Self so that she makes room for an open and exempt perception of her own and the client's expressions. In this place pre-judgements and programs are suspended. This is the *space of silence*. From this place she will be able to identify which kind of help the client may need and to be available to provide this help.

The space of silence

When the therapist goes to the *space of silence* two important consequences occur.

By staying connected with her Self, without splitting or conflicts, the therapist will stimulate a similar condition in the client. There is therefore *resonance* between them. It allows the therapist to find a truly receptive, compassionate, empathetic, and respectful attitude toward the client. The client, then, will hopefully be more able to express conflicts and contradictions, trusting that the therapist is there for her. In fact, this is the primary need of the client, as there is no right or wrong, good or bad in this place. Instead there is full acceptance of whatever the Self expressions are, allowing a space to their experience and integration.

The *space of silence* is crucial for allowing self-awareness and for enhancing the growth and maturation process, of both the client and the therapist.

The *space of silence* must be activated in a conscious way by the therapist.

In order to arrive there, the therapist must focus her attention on her breathing and its route through the back along the spinal medulla. Emphasis is placed on exhalation rather than inhalation (remember, you want to clear this space). After a few minutes of this procedure, silence and calm gradually replace the noise caused by the usual flow of thoughts from the Ego. There is where the therapist will find an empty space, cleared from all inconvenient interference, allowing her to receive information coming from the therapeutic relationship. As this flow of information is not under Ego control, you get a wide range and exempt quality of perception. Since this is a non-conventional type of breathing, it requires attention to keep it focused. This enhances *intention* and guarantees the therapist's full presence. At some point, the therapist will face, of course, resistance coming from the client, as defense mechanisms are activated by the Ego. Once this process is identified, the therapist will assist the client to comprehend as well as to overcome these forces, thus allowing freedom to expand and self-knowledge to grow. Distinguishing defensive behavior from the Self's true expression is part of the therapist's responsibility. To be able to accomplish this task, the therapist must be receptive to the flow of information within an egoless perception. This condition provides *essential wisdom* to come out for both client and therapist. From this perspective, the therapist is a partner who supports and accepts the truth of the client's self-expression in a journey of mutual expansion.

Conclusion

To be in the Space of Silence approximates a meditative condition and therefore, it requires a continuous practicing of one specific mode of breathing.

If this condition is often activated, the access to the Space of Silence will be progressively faster and natural.

For the therapist, the Space of Silence represents a condition of peace, where there is no room for expectations or directiveness of any kind. In fact, it can be felt as a blessing, as continuous ego pressure about ›doing the right thing‹ tends to cease.

Besides being an essential tool to be used in the therapy situation, the Space of Silence goes far beyond. Being there in the context of daily life can keep us safe from the intensive pressures we suffer from the world, which are the main reason for stressful and conflictual situations. Moreover, the Space of Silence creates for the person an introspective capacity, as well as more peaceful connections among people. This might help to clean the atmosphere for the planet too.

The Space of Silence is a space of discovery and health, wherein integration shapes connection between human beings and the Universe, creating a path of loving and harmonic energy.

References

Basso, T & Pustilnik, A. (2000): O Inconsciente emergente. Sao Paolo (Inst. Dinâmica Energética do Psiquismo).

Einstein, A. In: Vaughn F. (1985) (Ed.) Novas dimensões da cura espiritual. Sao Paolo (Ed.Cultrix / Pensamento).

Goleman, D. (1980): Perspectivas em Psicologia, realidade e o estudo da consciência. In: Walsh R. & Vaughn F. (1980) (Eds.): Além do Ego. Sao Paolo (Ed.Cultrix / Pensamento), pp. 32–39.

Jung, C.G. (1971): Psychological Commentary on Kundalini Yoga , Zürich (Spring Publications).

Pert, C. (1999): Molecules of emotion – Touchstone. In: Basso, T. & Amaral, M. (2000) (Eds.): Dermatomos. Sao Paolo (Inst.Cult. Dinâmica Energética do Psiquismo). Pp. 66–84.

Pierrakos, J. C. (1990): Energética da Essência. Sao Paolo (Ed Pensamento).

Reich, W. (1977): A função do orgasmo. Sao Paolo (Ed. Brasiliense).

Vaughn, F. (1985) (Ed.): Novas dimensões da cura espiritual. Sao Paolo (Ed.Cultrix / Pensamento). Pp. 19–36.

Maê Nascimento, lic.psychol.,
Rua Zaira, 245 – Pinheiros,
01252-060 São Paolo SP, Brazil,
E-mail: maenascimento@terra.com.br

Catharsis and Self-Regulation revisited: Scientific and Clinical Considerations[1]

Angela Klopstech

At this point in time, it is obvious that Bioenergetic Analysis can neither remain solely within the limitations of its original energy concepts, nor can it afford to lose its roots and become lost in the recent relational and process oriented approaches. In part, its viability will require that it expands its conceptual framework and cast a curious eye on the research from contemporary neuroscience. A continual reevaluation of old and integration of new concepts is necessary for surviving and thriving. This is also true in similar ways for the broader arena of body psychotherapy and much of my article will apply to other schools of body psychotherapy.

This article reevaluates and attempts to modernize an old concept, once crucial and revered, but now considered mainly inappropriate for clinical use. It explores whether the classical concept of catharsis, once a hallmark, still has a place in contemporary Bioenergetic Analysis; and if so, how it needs to be modified and elaborated. A reevaluation of the catharsis concept will also need to include a renewed understanding of self-regulation, the process catharsis does (or does it?) set in motion. For a while now, I have been interested in what roles high and low energetic charge, and the duality and balance between them, play as agents of change in the therapeutic process. The concept of catharsis is definitely a focal point in the debate about the significance and usefulness of therapeutic work with high vs. low charge.

My main thesis is that catharsis-promoting interventions and cathartic experiences can have an essential and well defined role in body psychotherapy, if and when a patient's high intensity cathartic experiences become

[1] This article is the translated and revised version of an earlier article published in German, in: Geissler, P. (Hg.) (2004): Was ist Selbstregulation? Giessen. (Psychosozial Verlag), S. 95–119.

integrated within the patient's self and are transitioned and extended into her everyday life – with its lower levels of intensity.[2]

In order to explore this thesis, I will begin by reviewing the role that catharsis has played in the evolution of psychotherapy as we know it today. Recent approaches from the neurosciences and theories of emotion, their research findings and their theories, shed new and helpful light on the concept of catharsis, and I will review and apply this material that is particularly relevant for an in-depth understanding of cathartic processes. I will then move on to define, describe and differentiate the various therapeutic processes involved in catharsis, and argue that an expanded concept of catharsis hinges on an expanded concept of self-regulation and the integration of cathartic experiences into the person and into her ongoing life. Finally, there will be some case-vignette notes to illustrate how the expanded concepts operate in actual clinical practice.

History and current state of affairs

From their founding years, through the humanistic psychology movement and then into the 1980s, a considerable number of body psychotherapies considered cathartic experiences an essential goal of therapy, leading to the widespread and sometimes exclusive use of catharsis-promoting interventions. They relied on cathartic experiences for a variety of reasons: It was dramatic, it was different, it seemed to show fast results, and at the end of the session the patients felt good (and the therapists powerful).

Then came a major paradigm shift, a rollback, relegating cathartic work to the slightly ›dirty‹ corner, with non-cathartic, i.e. softer interventions becoming the hallmark of the ›good therapist‹. And we are still living out this shift. This dramatic change is partially due to an attempted rappprochement to more mainstream therapy schools, particularly the relational theories and trauma related approaches, and partially – not to be underestimated – with political correctness and the ›feminization‹ of

[2] For stylistic brevity, I will employ the pronoun ›her‹ throughout this paper.

the therapy professions.[3] And at the same time, the self indulgent ›love affair‹ that some body psychotherapists had with their interventions and the often insufficient attention to the patient's words and the lack of relationship that used to go hand in hand with cathartic interventions, also played a significant role in this Hegelian counterreaction.

Historically, the use of cathartic methods, like hypnosis, and the therapeutic relevance of cathartic experiences dates back to Freud, Breuer and the beginnings of psychoanalysis. In their studies of hysteria, they emphasized the importance of affect and its discharge, arguing that remembering without affect is ineffective (Freud and Breuer 1970). But soon Freud cast cathartic methods aside in favor of other methods that he developed for bringing repressed and unconscious material to consciousness, i.e. the techniques of free association and the interpretation of dreams.

Reich considered the abandonment of catharsis a major error, picked up on Freud's original work on catharsis and made it a central aspect in his classic work on character analysis (Reich 1983). He expanded Freudian drive theory by introducing the concept of bodily defense mechanisms, the energetic counterpart to psychic defenses, thus developing an understanding of, and model for, the interaction of mind and body. Subsequently, he went on to develop not only new methods for treatment but a holistic model of human behavior, based on an intuitively appealing but scientifically questionable energy concept. This is not the place for a comprehensive assessment and critique of Reich's theories and ideas, and I will rather refer exclusively to the concepts that are relevant for our purposes.[4] Reich differentiated between the

3 It is probably more than accidental that the intense energy models were developed by men, at a time when male therapists dominated the therapy profession by sheer numbers. With the ›feminization‹ of the profession, relationship oriented models took center stage. Looked at with a Hegelian eye, the next movement should be towards a synthesis since both passion and relationship are central to human life.

4 Without doubt, Wilhelm Reich is one of the most influential but also one of the most controversial founding fathers of body psychotherapy. His ideas and treatment methods are at the root of a number of contemporary body-oriented therapy schools (prominent among them my own approximate professional home, Bioenergetic Analysis). Many of Reich's original ideas and their understanding and interpretation inspired an ongoing, often controversial discussion in our discipline. An extensive, detailed and differentiated overview is found in Cornell (1997) and Downing (1996).

neurotic and the genital (healthy) character, and his therapeutic treatment consisted of confronting and breaking through the character armor and dissolving the characterological and energetic resistances in order to reestablish the free flow of energy, unblock emotional impulses, and finally increase and deepen sexual experience.

Both, Reich's concept of the character armor that needs to be breached as well as his approach to treatment seem representative of his deep belief in the efficacy of cathartic methods. Once the armor was dissolved, he relied on the self regulating capacities of the human system (Reich 1983, p. 185):

> »As far as our clinical practice is concerned, there can no longer be any doubt that every successful analytical treatment, i.e. one which succeeds in transforming the neurotic character structure into a genital character structure, demolishes the moralistic arbiters and replaces them with the self-regulation of action based on a sound libido economy«.

Cornell, in discussing Reich's ideas, points out how much self regulation is seen by Reich as a direct consequence of catharsis, and is viewed as an automatic process that requires no further therapeutic effort and thus no therapeutic relationship for integration.

> »It seems that for Reich if the armor could be dissolved in session, the patient/organism becomes more self-regulating within his own somatic and energetic processes. The body comes more alive through the deepening of somatic and orgastic capacities. The relational ›work‹, relational change, comes through the genital embrace. The relational ›work‹, as such, occurs outside of the session« (Cornell 1997, p. 55).

Lowen based his formulations and development of the basic concepts of Bioenergetic Analysis clearly on a number of Reich's early ideas, particularly on his understanding of character and character analysis (Lowen 1958). His own understanding and use of catharsis though changed over time. Bioenergetic Analysis aims not just for feeling but for depth of feeling and has developed interventions to reach that goal, so cathartic work in the tradition of Reich was frequently employed in early Bioenergetic Analysis. Over time though, and at least in his later writings, Lowen changed his position and is surprisingly relational and process oriented, creating room for the role of the therapist and the necessity of integrative work.

> »However, the breakdown of ego defenses is not a legitimate goal of therapy. Such defenses are to be respected unless one can help the patient develop a more effective way of dealing with life stresses. The breakdown is only valid if it leads to a breakthrough. This involves the development of insight and integration of the new feeling into the personality« (Lowen 1980 p. 157).

While cathartic work played an important role for many body psychotherapies in the expansive and taboo-breaking sixties and seventies of the last century, it subsequently became the target of severe criticism. The use of cathartic experiences as agents of therapeutic change, growth and healing has steadily declined, as relational theories, trauma therapies and spiritual approaches have taken center stage. The bulk of the criticism points particularly to three potential problems: the possibility of retraumatization through the high charge and intensity involved in this work (Ogden & Minton 2000), the assumed short lived nature of insights originating from or conceived during cathartic experiences, and the danger of getting stuck in an ›addiction‹ where patients keep seeking out cathartic experiences for their feel-good potential. These criticisms and concerns are part of the more general debate about the role of and balance between energy and relationship, security and intensity, low vs. high energetic and emotional charge as therapeutic agents. The most comprehensive critique – albeit within the frame of a critical appreciation of the ideas of Reich and Lowen – comes from Downing (Downing 1996, p. 74):

> »In my mind the concept of catharsis suffers from the fact, (...) that many patients with early disturbances (whom we call borderline patients today) did not benefit from this treatment. The feelings that were set free were simply too overwhelming. (...) Some of the more stable patients that felt quite comfortable with strong emotions seemed to ›get stuck‹ in their cathartic outbreaks. As a result their affective explorations became stereotypical and slightly artificial«.[5]

[5] All translations from German into English are made by the author.

More generally, Downing thinks cathartic techniques are too provocative and aim too rapidly at a mobilization of intense feelings. I will respond to this criticism at a later point in this paper.

Very recently, the strong pendulum swing has been called into question, judging from some articles, conference contributions, and oral communication among colleagues. Cornell makes a case for »the reconsideration of the place of passion (...) within contemporary psychodynamic and body-centered psychotherapies« (Cornell 2003, p. 2). Pope considers both catharsis and containment to be relevant aspects of a healing process and argues:

> »Abuses of the catharsis phase have created an understandable avoidance of ungrounded and overwhelming use of emotional expression. Over-reliance on containment can also cause a stuck or incomplete process. Shifting a focus to appropriate expression and action can help people tend to unmet needs and complete unfinished processes, establish self-regulation, and healthy contact« (Pope 2000).

Klopstech, with her definition of ›energetic insight‹ creates a connection between deep emotional insights that accompany energetically and emotionally intense experiences with their cognitive-verbal representation of these experiences:

> »By ›energetic insight‹ I mean the cognitive insight that goes together with the actual physical and emotional experience of a shift inside the patient« and »The crucial component here is the almost-simultaneity of thought/feeling/body sensation. The simultaneous emergence and togetherness makes for the depth of experience and the experience of a shift inside« (Klopstech 2000, p. 60; 2002, p. 67).

An energetic insight often tends to include, with a little time lag, the more verbally symbolic brain, indicated by a verbal expression, a word or a sentence, but the resulting expression can also be physical, a deep sigh, a spontaneous gesture, or a smile.

What these recent contributions have in common is that they consider high intensity and deep feelings to have an important therapeutic impact, but they do not assume emotional health as an automatic and immediate consequence of the experience.

The decade of the brain and the renaissance of emotion theories

Essential contemporary contributions to the body psychotherapy topic of arousal/intensity/energetic charge as well as to the notion of self-regulation come from unexpected sources outside of body psychotherapy: neuroscience and emotion theories. Through modern imaging techniques, the neurosciences experienced a growth spurt during the nineties, the »decade of the brain« as Damasio (1994), one of its early and prominent proponents, named it. At around the same time, theories of emotion experienced a renaissance, characterized by a variety of overlapping and competing models as well as by research data.

The neuroscience of regulation processes

In a relatively new interdisciplinary endeavor »the best of modern science [converges] with the healing art of psychotherapy« (Siegel in Schore, 2003a, Preamble), and the results from neurobiology and neuropsychology are applied to understand and describe the origin and development of the self. What emerges from this meeting and overlapping of the various fields of neuroscience, infant research and psychotherapy theories is a complex, dynamic and holistic (brain-mind-emotion-body) view of the human being. The new discipline of interpersonal or affective neuroscience focuses on the basic role that brain bodily phenomena play in the process of change. This new knowledge and scientifically based understanding is of particular importance for us as body psychotherapists because it relates to the interplay of body, mind, emotion and interpersonal relations, which is at the heart of our therapeutic enterprise. Very recently, Bioenergetic therapists have started to consider the implications of neuroscience for their field (e.g. Koemeda 2004, Koemeda & Steinmann 2003, Lewis 2004, Resneck-Sannes 2003a, 2003b). And, for the first time from outside of body psychotherapy, the body is treated as an active and necessary protagonist for understanding development and process in psychotherapy, rather than being considered helpful at best and not essential at worst.

> »The brain is but one component of the complex system that is our body. We take in information and interact with the world through our bodies, and our bodies change with – and in some cases change – the cognitive and emotional processing« (Kutas & Federmeier 1998, p. 135).

This is certainly a statement in keeping with the Bioenergetic tradition!

What could the actual application and integration of neurobiological and neuropsychological findings into the therapeutic domain look like? One possible organizing frame is provided by the concept of self regulation and the critical relationship between affect regulation and the organization of the self. By far the most comprehensive work, an overview and evaluation of research data as well as a regulation theory and its application to psychotherapy and psychiatry, is provided by Schore in numerous articles and three remarkable books (1994, 2003a, 2003b). I will first present his view of the therapeutic relationship, then, more pointedly addressing our topic. I will focus on his regulation theory and his definition of self-regulation, both of which I view as neurobiological underpinnings for different aspects of cathartic processes.

At the heart of Schore's understanding of the therapy process is his claim that

> »...the therapeutic relationship can alter the patient's internal structural brain systems that nonconsciously and consciously process and regulate external and internal information, and thereby not only reduce the patient's negative symptoms but expand his or her adaptive capacities« (Schore 2003, p xvii).

He combines developmental research data of mother-infant interaction, neuroscience data and various psychoanalytic theories to describe the »psychobiological mechanisms by which the attachment relationship facilitates the development of the major self-regulatory structures in the infant's brain« (Schore 2003a, p.xiii). He then applies the developmental concept to models of the psychotherapeutic process: »If development fundamentally represents the process of change, then psychotherapy is, in essence, applied developmental psychology« (Schore 2003a, p.xvii). To make the shift from the maturing brain of infants to adult brains he uses neurobiological findings of continual right brain growth spurts throughout the lifespan »... the adult brain retains elasticity, and this elasticity, especially of the right brain that is dominant for self-regulation, allows for the emotional learning that accompanies a successful psychotherapeutic experience« (Schore 2003a, p. xviii).

For our agenda of revivifying the role of catharsis in Bioenergetic Analysis and body psychotherapy, Schore's regulatory theory and his definition of self-regulation are of particular interest. He distinguishes between two different forms of regulatory strategies, the conscious, voluntary and verbal control of emotional states lateralized to the left hemisphere and a nonverbal right-lateralized regulating function. Both sides of the brain share in the task of self-regulation, but they have different functions and different patterns of cortical-subcortical connections. The conscious left-lateralized regulation of emotion is a ›top-down‹ process (LeDoux 1996, p.172) with the upper and frontal parts of the cortex dominating subcortical activities. This is a more familiar regulation strategy, known as the concept ›that we change the way we feel by changing the way we think‹ and it is at the core of cognitive psychology and cognitive psychotherapy. Of more recent vintage, and relevant for the nonverbal, body-to-body communication between therapist and patient, is the research of the regulatory function of the right brain hemisphere. In general, the right hemisphere is dominant for the reception and expression of positive and negative emotions and for the coping with stress and uncertainty. More specifically this hemisphere is dominant for the implicit cognitive processing of facial, prosodic and bodily information that is embedded in emotional conversation. This applies to appraising interpersonal and social context, and it refers to such crucial nonverbal (and of course also verbal) therapeutic agents as attention and empathy. Thus, it encompasses information specific to the process of body psychotherapy, e.g. facial expression, quality of eye contact, voice, spontaneous gestures, touch and body contact. Contrary to the left hemisphere, information processing here is seen as a ›bottom-up‹ process: More specifically, Schore considers the right brain to be the biological substrate of the unconscious. He describes a hierarchical model of the self with cortical and subcortical structures of the right brain representing the unconscious and deep unconscious, and the orbitofrontal regions the preconscious.[6] In this view, as we shall see later on, cathartic processes, and the energetic insights they generate, can be understood as brain bodily ›bottom-up‹ processes, originating in the unconscious subcortical or cortical regions of the right brain, then emerging in the preconcious higher regions of the right cortex, and (most often) completing with a conscious and verbalized insight of the upper and frontal left cortex.

In addition, Schore provides a definition of self-regulation that includes Reich's understanding and is also more encompassing in that it makes room, even emphasizes the role of the interplay between therapist and patient. He distinguishes between an interactive and an autonomous, non-interactive mode and he postulates the flexible use of both modes as the hallmark of successful self-organization: »... self-regulation [is] the ability to flexibly regulate emotional states through interaction with other humans – interactive regulation in interconnected contexts via a two-person psychology – and without other humans – autoregulation in autonomous contexts via a one-person psychology« (Schore 2003, p. 259).[7] The source from which such flexibility evolves is a secure early relationship: »The adaptive capacity to shift between those dual regulatory modes, depending on social context,

6 Schore gives a detailed description of his understanding of the right brain as the biological substrate of the unconscious. For that matter, he reconceptualizes both Freud's structural model of the id, ego and super-ego, as well as the topographical model of unconscious, preconscious and conscious (Schore 2003a, p.250–277). I am using his topographical model here, where he refers to a »three-tiered vertically organized hierarchical limbic system, with the right orbital prefrontal cortex acting in an executive function for the right cortical hemisphere and its subcortical connections, that is for the entire right brain« (Schore 2003, p. 272).
Not relevant for this article, but of particular clinical interest are his ideas about the origin of narcissistic disturbances (Schore 2003a, p. 151–186) and his psychoneurological model of projective identification (Schore 2003a, p. 58–107).

7 One-person psychologies focus rather on the inner dynamic and the autonomy of the patient, while one- and one-half- and two-person-psychologies focus more on the relationship dynamic between patient and therapist. Compare Stark (1999) for a psychoanalytic and Klopstech (2000) for a Bioenergetically oriented description of these concepts.

emerges out of a history of secure attachment interactions of a maturing biological organism and an early attuned social environment« (Schore 2003, p.259). The importance and essence of any dyadic self-regulation, e.g. in the therapeutic dyad, is the expanded affect-regulatory capacity of the individual through the joint resources of the dyad, which serves as a »growth facilitating environment«, as Schore calls it.

Let us now look at Reich's understanding of self-regulation in the context of Schore's. It is Reich's prerogative to be the first theoretician and clinician to have formulated a holistic concept for the inherent human striving for self healing and self-regulation, and thus for the striving for full aliveness and vitality. At the same time, his concept was too constrained by his understanding of the therapy process and in all likelihood also because of the kind of person that he was. In the context of therapy, it was limited exclusively to autonomous self regulation and it viewed relational change purely as a result of this self-regulation, not as an integrated part of the broader therapy process. Within parent-child interaction though, Reich considered the capacity for ›orgonotic contact‹ by the parents to be an absolute necessity for the vitality and self-regulation of the child, but to my knowledge he did not draw any conclusions from this for adult self-regulating behavior.

In summary, taking together Schore's model of the therapeutic relationship, his dual hemisphere regulation theory and his understanding of self-regulation, and theoretically applying it to a moment-to-moment body psychotherapy process, his view of an optimal therapy process might look something like this: The empathic therapist is attuned and pays attention to the patient with her body and ›left ear‹. This involves both cortical and subcortical processing in the therapist's right brain: while the right amygdala acts as a sensor of unconscious affective communication, the right orbitofrontal cortex comes into play with the preconscious processes. It is here that amplification of affect takes place, within the intersubjective field, through the resonance of the therapist with his/her patient. This interactive regulation enables the patient to begin to verbally label the affective experience, first with an inner word that needs to be ›heard‹ by the therapist, then with a spoken word. It is here that the left hemisphere comes into play.

»The patient's affectively charged but now-regulated right brain experience can then be communicated to the left brain for further processing. This effect which must follow a right-brain-left-brain temporal sequence, allows for the development of linguistic symbols to represent the meaning of an experience, while one is feeling and perceiving the emotion generated by the experience« (Schore 2003a, p. 268).

Theories of emotion

Another source of important contributions is from recent theories and new research on emotion.[8] I will present three different yet overlapping theories and therapy approaches that are both representative of their field and relevant for our understanding of catharsis, cathartic processes and self-regulation. Greenberg, a researcher/therapist, is well known for representing the humanistic-experiential direction within emotion theory. His ›Emotion-Focused Therapy‹ considers intensity, expression and reflection to be major agents of change (Greenberg 2002). These three elements are, as we shall later see, the same agents that make cathartic experiences happen and cause their integration to be possible. Greenberg defines emotions in terms of cognitive, affective, motivational-behavioral schemes that produce a bodily felt referent. He describes the adaptive and meaning producing quality of emotions (Greenberg 2002, p. 2): »...emotions are a fundamentally adaptive resource«, and he stresses the communicative and interactive function of emotions »[they are] also a primary signaling system that communicates intentions and regulates interaction«. He then concludes »Emotion thus regulates self and other and gives life much of its meaning«. With regard to therapeutic interventions Greenberg reviews

8 For the various definitions of emotion, its differentiation from affect and reviews about its role in psychotherapy, compare Greenberg (2002), Greenberg & Safran (1989), Roth (2001). As body psychotherapists, and particularly as Bioenergetic therapists, our understanding of emotions tends to be based on energetic phenomena and I think it is important, if not necessary, for us to be well informed about how traditional psychology defines and understands emotions.

research that provides mounting evidence for the close connection between emotional arousal, depth of experience and emotional focus on one hand, and therapy outcome on the other. He argues »that high emotional arousal plus high reflection on emotional experience distinguish good and poor outcome cases, [at the same time pointing out that] (…) the expression and arousal of emotion can contribute to change (…) [but] the actual relationships among emotion, cognition, and somatic processes still remain unclear. Arousal and expression of emotion alone may be inadequate in promoting change« (Greenberg 2002, p. 13). On the basis of these findings he concludes that emotional arousal has to be combined with meaning construction and reflection, i.e. with a process of metabolizing and integrating high intensity experiences. Greenberg's work is particularly useful to body-centered psychotherapists since it is supported by research data and thus makes the therapeutic value of arousal (or in the language of Bioenergetic Analysis: energetic charge) academically respectable.

Another contribution relevant for our purposes comes from Traue (1998). At the core of his theory is the influence of emotional inhibition and repression on health and disease: »Emotion and health are two aspects of a psychobiological regulation where emotional inhibition plays a key role« (Traue 1998, p.14). Similar to Greenberg's approach he considers emotion to have a complex intrapersonal as well as interpersonal and communicative function. Taking this complexity into consideration he develops a multidimensional path model which describes the interconnection between inhibition and health. According to this model experience and expression of emotions have a crucial regulating function both for health and for social communication. Traue is within the academic tradition and has not developed his own therapy approach, but he provides a comprehensive overview of various therapy schools that promote expressivity, including a variety of body psychotherapies. In several instances he refers to the therapeutic efficacy of catharsis, stating:

> »The scarcity of studies regarding the efficacy of cathartic elements in psychotherapy is surprising, because every psychotherapy promotes the patient's emotional opening in expression and language. One could get the impression, that we are dealing here with an enduring aftermath of the psychoanalytical prejudgement of emotions, going hand in hand with the primacy of

> a culturally higher importance of cognition as opposed to the lowlife of the emotional ... Only an ›emotional change‹ in psychotherapy itself could rehabilitate catharsis as an essential therapeutic agent« (Traue1998, p. 376).

Yet another contribution, this time from the therapeutic domain, is provided by Fosha. With her ›Accelerated Experiential-Dynamic Psychotherapy‹ she develops a therapy model where »deep authentic affective experience and its regulation through coordinated emotional interchanges between patient and therapist are viewed as key transformational agents« (Fosha 2002, p.159). Experiencing, expressing and communicating deep affective states, Fosha calls them »core states«, as fully and viscerally as possible, is essential for achieving and maintaining emotional health.

> »Core affect comes to the fore when defenses are not in the picture (...). The visceral experiencing of core affect releases adaptive action tendencies associated with each emotion (...). Examples of the adaptive capacities that come to the fore when core affect is fully and viscerally experienced are: the strength and assertiveness facilitated by the full experience of anger, the clarity about one's basic needs and the resolve to address them often brought about by authentic self experience; or the capacity to trust, crucial to deepening intimacy, that comes with close and open relational experiences (...)[and going even further], the core state refers to an altered state of openness and contact, where the individual is deeply in touch with essential aspects of his own experience. In this altered state, the therapy goes faster, deeper, better: The patient has a subjective sense of ›truth‹ and a heightened sense of authenticity and vitality; very often, so does the therapist« (Fosha 2002, p. 160, 161).

It is the mutual regulation in the therapeutic dyad that fosters the full processing of core states. Like Schore, Fosha asserts that both individuals within a dyad have greatly expanded affect regulatory capacities resulting from the combined resources of the dyad. For the patient this means, that in expressing herself and receiving specifically tailored and attuned responses from the other, i.e. the therapist, the processing of core affect becomes complete.

Before taking a closer look at the different processes involved in catharsis, I will briefly review where these various research findings and therapy approaches converge, and how they relate to my considerations on catharsis. Greenberg, Traue and Fosha emphasize the importance of intensity and expression as therapeutic agents, with Greenberg focusing also on the after-the-fact reflection process. Intensity or high energetic charge and expression are hallmarks of cathartic processes, while reflection creates the path for their integration. Schore provides a model of a right-brain-left-brain process that can be understood as a neurobiological underpinning for the emergence of cathartic experiences and energetic insights. Schore and Fosha point to the enhanced self-regulating qualities for the patient through dyadic interaction, with Schore providing a neurobiological understanding for it. An expanded notion of self-regulation, including interaction between therapist and patient, is needed to make a plausible argument for a successful integration process after catharsis.

Catharsis

Catharsis: A definition

There is an absence of clarity and considerable confusion in the psychological and psychotherapeutic literature when it comes to understanding, applying and criticizing the concept of catharsis. As my next step I will attempt a working definition from which to make some clinically relevant distinctions between related, somewhat intertwined, but nevertheless different processes within the catharsis rubric.

›Catharsis‹ stems from the Greek word for cleansing, or purging, ›kathairein‹. Merriam Webster's Collegiate Dictionary defines catharsis as

> » a) a purification or purgation of the emotions (as pity and fear) primarily through art; b) a purification that brings about spiritual revival and release from tension; c) an elimination of a complex by bringing it to consciousness and affording it expression« (Merriam Webster's Collegiate Dictionary 1993, p. 181).

Given that Freud developed his ideas about catharsis inside the German language and that German is my mother tongue, I also will take into consideration a German language definition of catharsis. According to the Große Brockhaus, the quintessential German dictionary, catharsis is »the purification through emotional upset, according to Aristotle the impact of the [classical] tragedy, in psychoanalysis the abreaction of affect« (Der Brockhaus in einem Band 2003, p. 466).[9]

The English language domain emphasizes more the impact and effect of the purification, while the German language domain emphasizes the cause and the development of purification. Both definitions imply the *process* character of catharsis, though from different vantage points. In the latter instance the focus is on: »Where does it come from, how does it originate?« and in the first on: »Where does it go, what does it create?«[10] For our purposes of understanding the role of catharsis in the context of (body) psychotherapy, I will use an amalgam of both definitions. Together, these definitions account for the dramatic emergence into consciousness (insight): the process that brings something from the origin/ from the inside

---

9 Outside of the medical context of purification, the notion of catharsis was first used by Aristotle in his writings about the form and purpose of tragedy in his 'The Poetics'. Catharsis in dramatic art has always remained an ambiguous notion. It never became clear – and has been interpreted differently throughout the centuries – if Aristotle meant for catharsis to be applied solely to the drama itself or if he described its intended impact on the audience. Catharsis is the moment of insight and simultaneously the moment of dramatic and characterological reversal. In this moment the audience, and then that was the entire community, becomes an involved witness. That is the high point of drama, the catharsis.
Catharsis as a community defining and community specific phenomenon seems to have an archetypal quality. All cultures, religions and societies tend to have some form of ritual catharsis, e.g. confession in the catholic church, the Yom Kippur day in the Jewish faith and community, grieving rituals of the Mediterranean people, puberty initiation rites of some indigenous tribes, even the forced self criticism of the Mao-Tse-Tung Regime falls into this category; or presidential elections in the US may also belong here.
I am indebted to my friend Kathleen Dimmick, a dramaturg and theater director, for spending her time with me in repeated discussions on the topic.

10 The difference in emphasis is fascinating to me because it seems to reflect the cultural differences between the German speaking countries as part of the 'old world' and the US as ›the new world‹. Europeans are more tradition bound and tend to look at and rely on the past while Americans are rather action oriented and look to the future.

(emotional upset) to the outside/to the surface (expression). They also account for the quantitative and qualitative change (release of tension and spiritual revival). Catharsis is thus a concept which involves several distinct and different processes.

Cathartic experiences, the cathartic model, and processes by which catharsis is achieved

Cathartic experiences in body oriented psychotherapy are characterized by a discharge of tension; a spontaneous release of chronically tense holding patterns; a release that goes together with an undoing – dissolving, melting, breaking down – of characterological and energetic defenses; and by an emergence and breakthrough of feelings that aim for expression. This expression can take on very different forms: it can be a bodily expression like a gesture, or a vocal expression like crying or laughing, and/or it can be a verbal expression of a word, a phrase or a sentence. The result is a letting–go, a relief, a relaxation and a restoration; a release in the sense of a dissolving and in the sense of finding a solution; a freeing of impulses and words only dimly in the awareness and constrained and trapped in the preconscious, i.e. a »reorganization of impulses, action tendencies and inhibitions« (Geissler 1996, p. 222); an opening to the outer world of things and people, and an opening to the inner world of sensations, feelings, images and memories. Cathartic experiences can either catapult us or, more gently, give us a glimpse into a world that is new or anew, different from just before, from yesterday, from ›as usual‹. This world may be clearer or more colorful or more serene, and in the subjective experience it is always somehow ›better‹. When the strong waves of emotions subside to a flow that is smooth and tender, cathartic experiences are frequently followed by a small or big wonderment, by a peacefulness and peace of mind, and by a much slower thought process:

> »...the world looks clear and bright, the mind is awake yet slow, the feeling is sweet and the body at ease. For a while, feeling and thinking, inner and outer world are not in conflict with one another but in harmony; they follow the same rhythm and just are« (Klopstech 1991, p. 16).

With their »changed balance of impulse and resistance« (Geissler 1996, p. 222) and their »turn around of sense and meaning« (Traue 1998, p. 322) cathartic experiences become the ideal base for a new beginning.

And yet, there is reason for caution here: Cathartic experiences and cathartic insights can, but do not necessarily have to lead to a long term purification, restoration or change. They are the basis for a new beginning, even an ideal basis, but in themselves they do not yet constitute or guarantee an enduring change. They carry an immense potential for healing, but they are not the healing itself. They are meaningful, at times earth shattering experiences, but they are experiences in the here and now that need completion and integration. Without an appropriate integration into the self and everyday life of our patients, cathartic experiences frequently are the missed chances in therapy. This notion is congruent with Greenberg's research findings quoted earlier that arousal and expression of emotion have to be combined with meaning construction and reflection.[11]

A cathartic model, i.e. a catharsis-oriented therapy model would see cathartic experiences as the primary goal of therapy and seek them out deliberately. Implicit is the assumption, that cathartic experiences have such a dramatic, even magical effect that they automatically either instantly create a personality change or automatically set in motion a self regulatory process that carries the seed for enduring personality change. The new feelings, thoughts, body sensations and insights are seen as taking hold in the self without further outside help, and they get magically and automatically integrated into life outside of the therapy session, i.e. they result in more or less encompassing behavior changes in everyday life. Once catharsis is achieved, phoenix rises from the ashes. Therapists who essentially work in this therapy model may even get partial reinforcement for their approach, since the assumption of automatic self-regulation might at times apply for well functioning neurotic patients. We know how effective and resistant to extinction partial reinforcement is, and so, the cathartic model gets applied to all patients without diagnostic differentiation.

[11] Obviously, cathartic experiences and energetic insights overlap, but they do not quite describe the same thing. They both describe the same qualitative phenomenon, but they differ quantitatively: It would not be inaccurate to define energetic insights as »mini-cathartic experiences«.

Another crucial differentiation pertains to the process of *arriving at cathartic experiences*. To this day, it is often erroneously believed that cathartic experiences occur only when defenses are confronted and broken down. The specific interventions leading to this break down are either very active and fast-acting mobilization techniques or physical techniques relying on stress and pain as the major agent; in either case they involve an increase of intensity and energetic charge.

Mobilization techniques are, in fact, frequently a method of deliberately creating cathartic experiences. But they are only one method among many others, and are in no way a method appropriate for every patient. The diagnostic capacities of the therapist play an important role here. For well functioning neurotic patients who use a powerful muscular armor to avoid experiencing powerlessness, insecurity and abandonment, or who cannot let down and relax, this may be the method of choice. The emotional turmoil, and the release and relief that they may only experience through a strong energetic discharge, frequently opens the door to buried feelings of vulnerability and tenderness. The path is freed for a new beginning, a restructuring where assumed-and-defended-against deficits can become potencies, where ›weakness‹ can become vulnerability, insecurity can become self-reflection and a sense of abandonment can be turned outward to motivate a reaching out to others. What takes place here is a shift in consciousness, the dramatic change of sense and meaning that is described by Traue.

For a fragile self though, that struggles to keep a secure footing and its way in the world, the same intervention could be too overwhelming; the intervention may not lead to catharsis but to chaos, and rather than creating an opening, it can foster withdrawal and retreat from the world, or even dissociation.

In contrast to, but also in some sense complementary to mobilizing methods, are processes in therapy where the relationship between therapist and patient, or rather a momentary, particularized constellation of this relationship, can become the catharsis inducing factor. High energetic charge and emotional intensity plays an equally important role here, with the crucial difference being that the charge and intensity are generated interpersonally and not intra-personally. Body psychotherapy, with its abundance of body-to-body interventions has an extraordinary repertoire of techniques that can become carriers and facilitators for relational explorations. This happens if and when they are embedded in a proper context of transference and countertransference, in a ›co-created‹ relationship. The therapist provides either a corrective experience in the context of a one-and-a-half-person psychology or engages in an authentic relationship in the context of a two-person psychology. The cathartic experience comes about through the felt intensity of relating and the accompanying or resulting emotions and body sensations. This kind of cathartic process, if in the context of a secure and safe relationship, can be particularly helpful for the treatment of fragile patients, because the experience is taking place under a high arousal level and yet is not retraumatising. For trauma patients and patients with early disturbances, such cathartic experiences can play a key role in rekindling the faith in a ›good enough‹ world. Greenberg's research described earlier in this paper constitutes a scientific underpinning of these kinds of processes leading to catharsis.[12]

At this point, I will reiterate that therapeutic work with catharsis has its roots in Freudian Analysis. Contemporary psychoanalytic relational theories, though not using the word ›catharsis‹, seem to manifest an acute interest in an interactive concept of catharsis, of course within their own therapeutic frame that does not involve direct body-to-body communication. Stern, Tronick and the Boston ›Process of Change Study Group‹ describe »moments of meeting« between patient and therapist that create an »open space« where a »shift in the intersubjective environment creates a new equilibrium with an alteration or rearrangement of defensive processes« (Tronick et al.1998, p. 915), not only inside the therapeutic

[12] By no means do I want to give the impression that cathartic processes are a particularly suited method for working with trauma patients in general. They are not. But they are a possible method within the context of a safe therapeutic relationship. And for some patients, they actually help them develop a more robust ego and more tolerance for the world's turbulence. Trauma therapies that emphasize step by step procedures (e.g. Ogden & Minton 2000) or focus on guided imagination with continual stabilization (e.g. Reddemann 2001) or incorporate both features like EMDR (Shapiro 1995) have proven to be quite successful, both in research and in clinical practice. At the same time, I do want to make a case for ›somatic and interpersonal intensity‹ as an agent of change, when it occurs in a safe and supportive therapeutic dyad and diagnostically selectively used for some patients with early disturbances and PTSD.

relationship but also outside. Perhaps this is a rediscovery of catharsis, though not from the drive side but from a relational perspective.

And finally, there are cathartic experiences which are not consciously planned or and prepared for, but are just stumbled into. They can be generated by a »spontaneous condensation of relationship« within the therapeutic dyad. They can equally be generated by a »spontaneous energetic reinforcement« in the patient's body, e.g. evoked by a specific remark or gesture. Often, it is enough for the therapist to stay back and just let the cathartic process unfold, to be the witness of something precious and new unfolding; at other times it can be helpful or necessary for the therapist to accompany the process more actively by getting relationally involved or by deepening the energetic and emotional experience via technique.

Thus, there are actually a variety of processes by which catharsis can occur. They range from ›deliberately inducing catharsis as a therapeutic tool‹ at one extreme to ›recognizing catharsis and letting it happen as it occurs‹ at the other; from confronting interventions to corrective experience interventions; and they can occur in an autonomous context or in an interpersonal one.

Much of the bad press for catharsis in body psychotherapy stems from an oversight or oversimplification of its process character. There is often an insufficient or missing differentiation of the various components involved and/or a resulting confusion between therapy goals, therapeutic agents and treatment strategies. And, the variety of interventions and individually different treatment styles and approaches that body psychotherapists have creatively developed and appropriated over the last quarter of a century have not been viewed as integral instrumentarium for therapeutic work with cathartic processes; too often catharsis is only associated with an outdated and simplistic ›hit-kick-and-scream‹ approach.

After catharsis: The integration process

Another major criticism concerns the therapeutic process that follows cathartic experiences. Too often, there is no follow up process or if there is one, it consists more or less of a repetition of similar experiences, again and again. In my view it is the success or failure of the process following the original experience that determines the value of cathartic work in psychotherapy: Cathartic phenomena can have an essential role in body psychotherapy if and when a patient's high intensity cathartic experiences are integrated into the patient's self and are transitioned and extended into everyday life with its lower levels of intensity.

What does the process of integration and transitioning look like and how can and should the therapist move along and interact with this process? I have described how cathartic experiences with their freeing of impulses and feelings, rearrangement of defenses and creation of new meaning can serve as a basis for new behaviors and ways of being. I have also argued that this does not happen automatically, that self-regulation and integration are processes that need attention and tending. I want to refer again to Schore's definition of self-regulation and his description of an optimal therapy process. He describes self-regulation as flexible regulation, that can happen autonomously, i.e. with the patient relying on inner resources without help from the therapist, and it can happen as an interactive regulation within the dyad of patient and therapist. Both, the patient and the therapist need the capacity to be flexible, allowing them to switch, from moment to moment, between both regulation strategies.

For us as therapists, it requires attention and mindfulness, presence and acumen to adapt and respond to our patients' shifts. We need to listen with both our ›right‹ and our ›left‹ ear and look intuitively as well as with our analytical body readings in order to decide when we are needed as witness of a process and »only« provide attentive presence, space and time, or when we are called forth to become more active as regulators.

For the patient, mindfulness and attention to their bodily and emotional impulses, small or large, and their impulses for action play key roles both for autonomous and for interactive self-regulation.[13] In the autonomous mode, the patient is keenly, and often quietly, self aware of her inner processes. She swings with them and allows for them to build until things fall into place and a crystallization of the experience occurs,

[13] Mindfulness is an ancient Buddhist meditation and healing concept, that has found its way into the western therapeutic arena, accordingly modified e.g. as ›Focusing‹ in Gendlin's work (Gendlin 1978), or as ›Tracking‹ in Levine's work (Levine 1997) and Ogden & Minton (Ogden & Minton 2000).

either as a sentence, most often an ›enabling sentence‹, or as a completion of an impulse for action. The impulse may take the form of a spontaneous reaching for the hand of the therapist – now the patient is ready to reach out into the world of people. Or, rather than being a movement just of the hand or the arm, it may be a movement of the whole body into the room, an expansive bodily movement that entails greater ownership of space. Or the patient's inner process brings forth a sentence that captures the cathartic experience simultaneously with a new meaning. These sentences tend to show the way to future actions. I call them ›crystallization sentences‹ or ›enabling sentences‹ or ›power sentences‹. Typical enabling sentences for the first process just described could be: »My God, somebody is there for me! I just need to dare reach out« or for the second example »I am here, I am really here and this is my place!« Dyadic interaction can help with further integration, by the therapist listening with a »resource-oriented ear« (Reddemann 2001, p. 18) and looking with resource-oriented eyes. The therapist might offer herself for physical interaction, or offer a (body) experiment or a verbal exchange for further exploration of possible actions.

If we perceive that autonomous self-regulation is weak, we may be able to ›hear‹ a sentence that is yet inchoate for the patient or we may have a hunch about a gesture that is not born yet, and we can formulate the sentence or help the birth of the gesture, thus indicating, not leading the new way. Dyadic interaction builds a bridge here: From an ›open space‹ into the new land of a completed gesture and action, or new meaning and behavior. This is interaction at a low arousal level, at low charge. As body psychotherapists we also have the added advantage of more active interventions. Particularly, we can offer our direct somatic presence in the form of body-to-body-interaction and thus to direct right-brain-to-right-brain-interaction. The bodily interaction may ›only‹ consist of positioning ourselves in relation to the patient, standing or sitting, closer or further away, more to the right or the left, available for eye contact and directly in the field of vision or more to the side. The physical interaction can also consist in adapting the rhythm of our breathing to the patient's rhythm, creating an intimate physical connection without direct body contact. Or, in direct body contact, we can offer our helping hand, our supportive arm or we can actually ›back‹ our patient. And we can help our patients to get on their feet, first literally then metaphorically.

At this point I will describe a specific intervention that can be used in a variety of contexts, taking on different meanings within each specific context, and that has proven particularly useful in integrating cathartic experiences (Klopstech 1991). It is a simple, almost meditative intervention, that provides a somatic experience of unfolding, continuation and process. I ask the patient ›to walk slowly and mindfully‹, and with each step, have her feet make conscious contact with the ground, rolling the sole from heel to toe with the knees unlocked to encourage letting down and experiencing the presence and support provided by the ground. The head can rest easy on top of the spine, the eyes can relax and, without effort, look at what's to be seen in the outside world. After a while, forward motion, emotions and thoughts blend into a rhythm and enabling sentences emerge: »life goes on, step by step« or »things will work out, one step at a time«« or »this is my way« etc. The felt forward-movement gives an experience of being grounded and simultaneously being in motion. This provides a sense of harmony with oneself and, at the same time, a sense of present and future, of being in process, more a right brain phenomenon, while the metaphorical sentence reflects the experience consciously and verbally, a left brain activity. Anchoring an experience in the self and transitioning it into everyday life, one step at a time makes sense energetically and emotionally. There are many opportunities for dyadic regulation here: I may witness and accompany with my voice and with words, or I may actually physically accompany the person. I may move towards my patient and we meet. At times we walk together, being on the same path for a while, until walking alone comes more easily. We may walk hand in hand, or just next to each other, looking out at the small world of my office, perhaps exchanging what we each see.

This integration is of a short term nature. It follows pretty much right after catharsis has occurred, making use of the release of tension, the let down of defenses and the resulting clearing. The same intervention, though, can be used for long term integration and transition. The felt forward-movement is an intervention involving the whole body and self, replete with metaphors like ›moving ahead‹, ›ongoing movement‹, ›life goes on‹, ›to meet halfway‹, ›talking the talk and walking the walk‹, and can be viewed and used as a way of ›checking in‹ with the integration process. In general, the cognitive processing changes with time, different yet related aspects and enabling sentences emerge, manifesting increased self-regulation and at the same time increasing further self-regulation. The physical process may change, too. Insecure, tentative steps may transition to more secure footing over time, small steps may become more daring and longer while giant steps prone to wobbling may shrink to a manageable size. How well the physical and the cognitive processes match, the degree of balance between the body and mind, is an indicator of the quality of the integration process.

The high intensity and drama of catharsis may overshadow the fact that everyday life takes place on a lower level of intensity and excitement and that high intensity experiences do not automatically and magically integrate. The ongoing integration process needs continued attention and ›care‹. The therapist has the task of holding the integration and transitioning processes in the dyadic consciousness, i.e. to keep it alive in the therapeutic process without becoming responsible for it or controlling it. For some patients integration is easier for several reasons. They have more access to their inner life, are more action oriented in general, or are surrounded by people that help and support their endeavor – interactive self-regulation outside of therapy. For others, it is harder because the memory of the cathartic experience and its feeling of well-being are ethereal, and the new behaviors keep slipping out of reach. In this case, interactive self-regulation in the growth facilitating environment of the therapeutic dyad becomes even more important.

Clinical moments

The following are examples of cathartic processes drawn from therapy. Some differ with regard to the processes leading up to a cathartic experience, others with regard to the integration processes, and still others differ in both regards. These segments are not case studies or even vignettes since they are cursory and moment-focused. They rather have the character of snapshots, embedded in and enriched with some background information. I call them clinical moments.

Classical mobilization

This clinical moment takes place during the sixth session. The patient is a rather stiff, shy woman in her late thirties with held back aliveness which at times breaks through in an unexpected laughter. Her main presenting problem is her social awkwardness, particularly in stress situations, resulting inevitably in sudden nausea occasionally accompanied by vomiting. At this point in her therapy we are both aware of the importance of movement for her. She finds it much easier to talk with me while walking around my office, moving her arms as she talks. From the context of this and previous sessions, I propose an experiment: to lie down on the mattress and move her arms and legs strongly in a kicking motion while at the same time using the word ›I‹. It is as if a dam breaks: her whole body becomes involved in a series of increasingly strong, loud and determined ›I‹ statements leading up to a triumphant finale. After a long pregnant silence she opens her eyes and her first words are »I see colors. Everything here in the room is so much more colorful … three dimensional … clearer …«. As she looks at me, she blushes and gives words to what I also experience in this moment: »You feel so much closer now«. I tell her that my experience matches hers and ask her if she likes the feeling of being closer. This brings her back to the discovery of her new self and she starts thinking about whom *she* would like to be closer to in her outside life and which ›I‹ sentences she can find to express her wish to her beloved ones and other people in her life. She experiences herself as more engaged than usual and the world as more exciting and less thwarting. During the following sessions she frequently stops herself, takes a good look at me and tunes inside, checking out if and when she wants more closeness with me. She coins the phrase »Now I want to check in with my ›closeness-I‹«. In her life she starts feeling less awkward and instead more carefree and easygoing.

Somatic and interpersonal intensity

The following cathartic situation occurs after three months of therapy. The patient is a forty year old woman. At this point in therapy, we are both aware that a big part of her life consists of fighting, starting with her family of origin in South America and continuing here in the US where she started out as an immigrant without a Greencard, rising to become a well regarded physician. Her fighting mentality is manifested in a hard muscled body with the strong jaw of a warrior. Her overdeveloped calves and thighs insure that nobody will push her over! She feels understood and accepted in the relationship with me, and so I can offer her an intervention, deliberately not telling her its purpose so as not to influence her reaction. I tell her that I want to carry her on my hands and explain the technique. Her immediate reaction is surprise, disbelief and the concern that she will be too heavy ... then an apprehensive nod of her head. I lie down on the floor, on my belly with my arms extended forward and my palms turned upward. She slowly starts to move onto my hands with the soles of her feet. I can feel in my hands how she is letting down more and more, giving me more of her weight, relying on me to support her. She tells me how relieving this feels to her. Then I hear a deep sigh and she breaks into a sobbing that shakes her whole body ... but she remains on my hands ... crying for a long time. What comes to her mind when the sobbing abates is something she has not realized before: how much she criticizes and bosses her husband around with sentences like »Why didn't you do ...«. She is horrified. I say to her »demands harden and wishes soften«. She is quiet ... I ask her to slowly leave my hands and to move back onto her feet. She experiences the ground as softer than before, with more give. I ask: »The way you would like to be?« The next session she tells me that during the past week she made a point of asking her husband rather than demanding and that she felt less exhausted than usual. »Also« she says half embarrassed, half fascinated »sex was much better«.

Spontaneous condensation ... and somatic and relational intensity

The next cathartic situation happens after half a year of therapy, unplanned and initially not deliberately encouraged by me. The patient, a tall but inconspicuous woman in her mid-forties, is married to an unreliable and flaky husband; he wants more space in the relationship, she wants more closeness and reliability. She comes from a large family whose roots go back to the first American settlers and whose men played an important role in American politics in the last century. We spent the last sessions dealing with how unimportant she felt in her famous family but also how this guaranteed her a place, albeit a marginal one, in the family. This is a difficult topic for her!

She becomes energetically ›smaller and smaller‹ as she talks. She bites her lips, lets her head hang, breaks eye contact and falls silent. I offer her the opportunity to hit on a foam cube with the words: »I am here and this is my place«. This is obviously not a helpful intervention and the hitting stays mechanical. I change my position, placing myself next and close to her so that she can see me from the corner of her eye and say »I would like to know what you *want* to say ... what *you* want to say«. Her head flings up and she cries out violently »I don't know where to go«. I respond »to me, now, today, here, to me ... with your eyes to me«. While she keeps sobbing, we spend the remainder of the session turned towards each other, half sitting, half lying on the mattress; she opens her eyes and I am there with mine, she closes her eyes and I stay there with mine and I am there with my eyes when she opens hers again. Now her words start to flow, many memories come up and find their way into words and sentences, memories of her family and what she had wished for; how much she wanted to be picked up by her father, wanted to sit on her mother's lap, how much she wanted a ›normal family life‹. She starts blossoming as we talk, our eyes still locked. At our next meeting she brings in several pictures that she painted after the last session. They are all colored drawings showing herself and her immediate family members. She either wears a red or yellow dress, always being center stage, on her mom's lap, her dad's arm, hand in hand with her brother. While she keeps painting pictures for the next sessions, bringing them in, showing me her fantasized and painted ideal family life, and while I listen to her and look at her in our therapy sessions, her actual family life of today starts improving. The relationship with her husband undergoes a significant change; she pulls him more down to earth and more into responsibility for the ongoing business of their daily lives. At the same time she becomes more open to his wishes for more individuality and boundaries in the relationship. They learn, together and from each other, to wish, to demand, to give in, to negotiate.

Concluding remarks

Reflection on the therapeutic effect of catharsis is more than 2000 years old. It started with Aristotle, who ascribed – in contrast to his teacher Plato – to passion and catharsis the effect of promoting insight, of increasing the power of reasoning rather than squelching it. And to this day, artists, philosophers, theologians and anthropologists have struggled with the concept, each from their own vantage point and with their own agenda. For me, psychotherapy, which is a relatively young discipline can only profit both as an applied science and as an art, by sitting at the table with these long established disciplines and by becoming involved in the ongoing debates about the ever changing nature and meaning of ancient but enduring ideas and concepts. Catharsis is one such concept.

References

Aaron, L. und Anderson, F. S. (1998): Relational Perspectives on the Body, Hillsdale NJ (The Analytic Press).

Bockhaus GmbH Leipzig (2003): Der Brockhaus in einem Band, 10.Auflage, Mannheim (Augsburger Druck und Verlagshaus), p. 466.

Cornell, B. (1997): If Reich Had Met Winnicott: Body and Gesture. In: Energy & Character 28, p. 50–60.

Cornell, B. (2003): The Impassioned Body: Erotic Vitality and Disturbance. To be published in: British Gestalt Journal.

Damasio, A. R. (1994): Descartes' Error. New York (Grosset/Putnam).

Downing, G. (1996): Körper und Wort in der Psychotherapie. Leitlinien für die Praxis. München (Kösel).

Downing, G. (2000): Emotion Theory Reconsidered. In: Wrathall, M & Malpass, J. eds.: Heidegger, Coping and Cognitive Science, MIT Press, Vol 2, p.245–270

Freud, S. & Breuer, J. (1970): Studien über Hysterie (Original publication 1895). Frankfurt a.M. (Fischer).

Fosha, D. (2002): The Dyadic Regulation of Affect in Psychotherapy: A Psychodynamic-Experiential Integration, In: USABP Conference Proceedings. p. 159–177.

Gendlin, E. T. (1978): Focusing. New York (Bantam Books).

Geissler, P. (1995): Psychoanalyse und Bioenergetische Analyse: Im Spannungsfeld zwischen Abgrenzung und Integration. Frankfurt a. M. (Peter Lang).

Geissler, P. (1996): Neue Entwicklungen in der Bioenergetischen Analyse. Frankfurt a.M. (Peter Lang).

Greenberg, L. S. (2002): Integrating an Emotion-Focused Approach to Treatment into Psychotherapy Integration. In: Journal of Psychotherapy Integration, Vol 12, No 2, S.154–189.

Greenberg, L. & Safran, J. (1987): Emotion in Psychotherapy: Affect , cognition and the Process of Change. New York (Guilford Press).

Klopstech, A. (1991): A Backdoor to Grace: the Best We Can Offer. In: The Clinical Journal of the Institute for Bioenergetic Analysis, Vol 4, Nr.2, p.16–31.

Klopstech, A. (2000): The Bioenergetic Use of a Psychoanalytic Conception of Cure, Bioenergetic Analysis, Vol 11, Nr.1, p.55–66.

Klopstech, A. (2002): Modelle Therapeutischen Handelns: Der psychoanalytische und der bioenergetische Weg. In: Koemeda-Lutz, M. (Hg.): Körperpsychotherapie – Bioenergetische Konzepte im Wandel. Basel (Schwabe), p.61–74.

Koemeda, M. (2004): Die relative Bedeutung von Kognition, Affekt und Motorik im psychotherapeutischen Prozess – eine bioenergetische Perspektive. Lecture held at the Vienna Symposium *Psychoanalyse und Körper*.

Koemeda-Lutz, M. & Steinmann, H. (2004): Implikationen neurobiologischer Forschungsergebnisse für die Körperpsychotherapie unter spezieller Berücksichtigung der Affekte. In: Koemeda, M. (Hg.) (2004): Neurowissenschaften und Psychotherapie. Der Mensch: ein Thema, zwei Welten. Psychotherapie Forum (12) No.2.

Kutas, M. & Federmeier, K. D. (1998): Minding the body. In: Psychophysiology 35, p.135–150.

LeDoux, J. (1996):The Emotional Brain. New York (Simon & Schuster).

Levine, P. (1997): Waking The Tiger: Healing Trauma. Berkeley (North Atlantic Books)

Lewis, R. (2004): Listening with the Limbic System. In: Bioenergetic Analysis, Vol 14, No1.

Lowen, A. (1958): The Language of the Body. New York (McMillan).

Lowen, A. (1980): Fear of Life. New York (MacMillan).

Merriam Webster, Inc. (1993): Merriam Webster's Collegiate Dictionary. Tenth Edition, Springfield, MA. p. 181.

Ogden, P. & Minton, K. (2000): Sensorimotor Psychotherapy: One Method for Processing Traumatic Memory. In: Traumatology, Vol VI (3).

Pope, T. (2002): Containment and Catharsis, USABP Konferenz 2002, unveröffentlichter Konferenzbeitrag.

Reddemann, L. (2001): Imagination als heilsame Kraft. Stuttgart. (Pfeiffer bei Klett-Cotta).

Reich, W. (1983): Charakteranalysis. New York (Farrar, Straus, Giroux).

Resneck-Sannes, H. (2003): Psychobiology of affects: Implications for a somatic psychotherapy. In: Bioenergetic Analysis, Vol 13, No1, p111–122

Resneck-Sannes, H. (2003): Bioenergetics: Past Present And Future. Unpublished manuscript presented as lecture at the biannual international Conference of the International Institute for Bioenergetic Analysis, San Salvador, Brazil

Roth, G. (1994): Das Gehirn und seine Wirklichkeit, Frankfurt. (Suhrkamp)

Schore, A. (1994): Affect Regulation and the Origin of the Self: The Neurobiology of Emotional Development. Hillsdale NJ (Erlbaum).

Schore, A. (2003a): Affect Regulation and the Repair of the Self. New York (Norton).

Schore, A. (2003b): Affect Dysregulation and Disorders of the Self. New York (Norton).

Siegel, D. (2003a): Preambel. In: Schore, A. (2003a): Affect Regulation and the Repair of the Self. New York (Norton).

Stark, M. (1999): Modes of Therapeutic Action. Northvale, NJ. (Jason Aronson).

Traue, H. (1998): Emotion und Gesundheit. Heidelberg (Spektrum).

Tronick, E. Z., Bruschweiler-Stern, N., Harrison, A.M., Lyons-Ruth, K., Morgan, A.C., Nahum, J.P., Sander, L.W., Stern D.N. (1998): Non-Interpretative Mechanisms in Psychoanalytic Therapy. Int. J. Psycho-Analysis. 79, S. 903–921.

Dipl.-Psych. Dr. Angela Klopstech,
40–50 East Tenth Street, #1c,
New York, NY10003, USA,
Tel/Fax: 212–2603289,
Email: klopkoltuv@aol.com

Review of »Honoring the Body – the Autobiography of Alexander Lowen«

Philip M. Helfaer

> »The fulfillment that life and therapy offer is the ability to be fully true to one's self. That self for me is the bodily self, the only self we will ever know. Trust it, love it and be true to yourself« (Lowen 2004, p. 243).

For as long as I've known him, he has been ›Al‹ for nearly everybody who meets him. He has a simplicity, directness, and lack of pretension that invites us to address him in the personal form. From this man who has been so important to the Bioenergetic community and so significant in many of our lives, we now have his autobiography. It is essential reading for anyone who practices Bioenergetic Analysis, and it is a significant and useful contribution for anyone interested in the field.

Besides Dr. Lowen, we have Robert Glazer to thank for its publication. He helped Al complete the book, edited and published it. I saw a version of the manuscript prior to Glazer's collaboration on the project, and I can attest that the material in the manuscript I read corresponds in content, style, and tone with the material in the published book. The outcome is an excellently developed, well organized whole. As with all of Lowen's writing, it can be read with, perhaps, deceptive ease.

I take the publication of his autobiography as a celebration of his life, and reviewing it, for me, is an honoring of the man. Alexander Lowen is one of those fortunate men whose life and work touched and benefited many other people. He is therapist, mentor, teacher, writer, and developer of Bioenergetic Analysis. He was the student of Wilhelm Reich who brought Reich's work back to earth and made it widely available in the form of a treatment modality, a view of the human condition, an organization, and a training program. In *Honoring the Body*, Lowen speaks with unvarnished honesty about how he sees his own shortcomings. His accomplishment, regardless, is impressive and praiseworthy.

There is one dominant feature of the book that will stand out for every reader. This story of his life is the story of the development of Bioenergetic

Analysis. Lowen was totally dedicated to his work. His Introduction is framed by two sentences.

> »The underlying purpose of Bioenergetic Analysis has always been to heal the mind-body split. ... I've dedicated my life to the pursuit of healing my own mind-body split and the pleasure of the life of the body« (pp. 7, 10).

These two sentences are indicative of the way in which his personal story and Bioenergetics are intertwined. The personal background of Part One leads up to the meeting with Reich. What follows is his therapy with Reich, and his finding himself through the affiliation with Reich and Reich's work. From here, he goes on to become a Reichian therapist and then to found Bioenergetic Analysis. Subsequent sections revolve around an account of his books, the basics of Bioenergetics, and the development of the International Institute for Bioenergetic Analysis. Personal crisis always goes hand in hand with a crisis in his conception of Bioenergetics and a subsequent deepening of that conception.

The story of his own healing is a sub-theme. There are other sub-themes as well, the most important of which, of course, is the tender and touching story of his courting, marrying, and subsequent life with his beloved wife, Leslie. The happiest years of his life, he says, were those just after their marriage when they were living in Greenwich Village, New York City. This was before medical school and before Bioenergetics.

After returning from medical school in Switzerland, work dominated his life, as it did for Reich. He did better than Reich, however, even in the years when Bioenergetics was a growing field, in maintaining his capacity for pleasure and making time for it. Skiing, sailing, and his beach house were enjoyments and passions. He also took pleasure in travels, especially when Leslie accompanied him. He enjoyed workshops in which a camaraderie developed in a setting of natural beauty where there was simple good food, local music, and dancing.

More than simply work, however, a deeply felt mission dominated Lowen's life, above and beyond everything else.[1] He felt driven by it. He

[1] See pages 92, 154, 208, 217.

saw that it left him in conflict with colleagues. He also deeply believed in it. At the same time, again, he could self-critically associate his sense of mission with what he perceived as his ›narcissism‹. Under this heading he included his wish for fame. Further, he says,

> »I have felt that I absorbed some of his (Reich's) messianic feeling. (...)
>
> And yet I could always justify my position. Wasn't this that I was doing an important contribution to mankind? Yes, and I still believe so« (p. 92, p. 208).

As much as he believed in it, he was never quite comfortable with his mission. He ties it in to his struggles in other ways. »I felt helpless, and yet I couldn't give up my struggle. I couldn't accept the idea of failure« (p. 208). He says that at age sixty-six he began his struggle to get free and have more peace and joy (p. 208), but it was almost twenty years later before he was able to resign as director of the Institute he had founded (p. 210). Then, »I felt like a free person«.

I see here a tragic aspect to Lowen's character. He seems never to have separated out his sense of mission as a valid and good part of himself from other aspects of himself, ›narcissism‹, about which he was very self-critical. Surely, it is possible to have a mission one strongly believes in without it being an expression of narcissism.

For those of us for whom Al has been an important figure in our lives, any reading of his autobiography will be colored by our own autobiographies. I, myself, found the story and the voice very familiar – up to a point. In *Honoring the Body*, Lowen tells of his life struggles, both personal and as founder and developer of Bioenergetic Analysis. In reading about these, I hear another voice, one that is not so familiar, running along side of the more familiar one. This is the voice of insecurity and self-criticism, at times a voice verging into despair, at times expressed in painful somatic symptoms. It is the voice emerging out of crisis and a sense of failure. It is the voice longing for freedom, peace, and joy.

From this voice I gained insight into my own life journey and a deeper understanding of Bioenergetics, and I believe others may too. In addition, in listening to this voice, I found help with a basic set of questions. What does Lowen mean by ›the mind-body split‹, and how does he himself experience it? How have these experiences influenced the development of Bioenergetic Analysis? I approached *Honoring the Body* with these questions.

Within *Honoring the Body* there are several stories. There is the remarkable American story of the child of immigrant parents who makes good by dint of wits, long hard work, and determination. There is the story of the lonely child of neurotic, unhappy parents, who becomes the sexually tormented adolescent and youth, who fights his way toward health, love, and a life devoted to helping others along the same path. There is the story of the young man whose ›identity moratorium‹ lasts into his early thirties who finds a trusted, powerful mentor. The mentor accepts the young man into his fold and provides the environment and rites of passage from which the young man emerges to find his own masculinity, adulthood, and identity. He then moves out into the world to work, love, marry and found his own family, personal and professional. There is the story of the ›empire builder‹, whose efforts, conflicts, and struggles cost himself considerably. There is the story of the intellectual with a remarkable, constant outpouring of books and articles over many years, all deeply probing »the nature of the human condition«, as he would call it. There is, of course, a story of love and romance, his marriage to the lovely woman he »had to marry«. Finally, there is the story of the seeker whose lifetime is guided by a spiritual practice. His quest is for healing, fulfillment, and real joy. His method is the devoted exploration of the energy of the body and of grounding. Overall, here is a story of a long life, well lived, and lived to the full.

Then, there is the story of his relationship with his mother. She seems to have been a terribly frightened, anxious person, quite lost, alone, without a secure connection to her husband, without much sense of self, looking to her son for connection and security. Her effect on her son's, Alexander's, development left him with life-long struggles. Out of his mother's impact on his development emerges much of the feeling and meaning that went into Lowen's sense of the mind-body split. He shares a brilliant and painfully incisive account.

> »Most of my life I have worked to restore the body to the central position in the hierarchy of the personality. It is the ground of our being and the basis for our sexuality. Why did I not make my position clear when I created the Bioenergetic approach to the understanding and treatment of emotional problems?

> The answer lies in my personality structure, which is split. My identification with my body has been on the level of survival and pleasure, whereas my identification with my mind was on the basis of success and superiority. It was only on the level of my intellectual ability that I could prove that I was as good, if not better than others. This need to prove my superiority stemmed from a deep feeling of humiliation associated with my bodily functions and from my identification with my mother in her contempt for the body. Although the therapy with Reich lessened this identification with my mother, it did not ground me enough in the body. The reason for this was very simple but not clear at the time. Reich was also a thinker, albeit a great one who used his intellectual ability to overcome his own deep feelings of inferiority and humiliation relative to his father and older (sic) brother. My egotism was big (»I want to be famous«). His egotism was even bigger. He was a ›great man‹. (...) (M)y egotism got in the way of developing Bioenergetics as a solid foundation for understanding the human dilemma« (p. 217).

Underlying his long career is his life-long struggle to get free of a very destructive relationship with his mother. Her negative, even cruel, way of relating to her son around bodily functions and his masculinity left him with a deep bodily sense of shame and humiliation. At the same time, his own real experience showed him that his body is his only source of well-being, comfort, and pleasure. Framing his split in stark, simple, bold terms – body versus mind – enabled him to grapple with the archetypal mother and emerge with his life.

Fortunately, he was intellectually gifted, and he used his gifts to move through his education with ease. He became aware of his use of his intellect in his adaptation, his effort to get along despite fear, insecurity, aloneness, lack of a strong sense of self, and humiliation. If he was driven in his efforts, he can hardly be blamed. His fight for survival was deadly serious. Fortunately, again, he had the energy to carry it off.

His judgment of himself in the lines above is harsh, even merciless. Elsewhere, he refers to the ›tyrannical ego‹, the ego we are ›slaves‹ to, the ego that is a ›dictator‹, all of which might better be termed an ›ego-ideal‹ in the service of a ›super-ego‹ (p. 128).

What Alexander, that mother's son, never had, was an empathic ear for the humiliation and a compassionate interpretation of ›superiority‹ as the natural effort to rise above humiliation. Thus he came to distrust the intellect, as he felt it becomes a tool to distance from the body. However, ›rising above‹ is the natural energetic adaptive response to humiliation, charging the brain is a result. The ›criminal‹ is not the brain, it is the original ›insult‹. It is very difficult to let down from such injuries, especially on one's own, and it is probably a life-long process even under the best of circumstances. So it is that Lowen returns again and again to his quest to be grounded, to connect to the original mother, Mother Earth, as the only support, compensation, and cure available for the destruction wrought by his mother.

At age twenty-eight, Lowen faced a crisis which he met in a characteristic way (p. 30). He realized he was depressed. He resolved the depression by doing exercises after work. He wanted more than ever to find a way to make a living through being in his body. He felt his split. He could be ›special‹ through his intellect (p. 29), but only through his body could he find pleasure and a good feeling. Al had sought out physical activities, sports and games of all kinds, as his refuge and salvation from the time he was a child, playing in the streets of Harlem in New York City, then a largely Jewish community. From five to fifteen, »the street was the center of my life« (p. 19). In high school and college there were handball and basketball, later tennis and skiing. He was an athletics coach for adult summer camps during his twenties. The impression of his sheer physical energy and activity is strong. His experience with Reich confirmed his own instincts and predilections. Relief from our insecurities, anxieties, and neurotic conflicts can be found through the body, specifically, as he learned in his experience with Reich, freeing the energy of the body. The ›mind‹ may mean living the life of the intellect, but this is not masculine, and it is an effort at superiority, an effort to realize the ego values of a culture divorced from nature and the body. For Lowen, these remain deeply held convictions. Throughout *Honoring the Body* Lowen refers to a deeply felt insecurity, a wish to build the foundation for a stronger sense of self, the longing to be freed from sexual shame and torment, and the quest for a stronger sense of masculinity and the ability to love. These needs seemed to have been remarkably well fulfilled in his therapy with Reich. I found one of the most touching passages in the book to be this tribute to Wilhelm Reich.

> »So much of the power of Reich's therapy was in the strength of his personality and the strength of his being. Reich was brilliant and knew his ideas were right. I drew energy from Reich, and his courage and his energy gave me the trust to face the sexual repression and shame that I had been raised with. In the two and a half years of therapy I did with Reich, I was able to feel and surrender to my body in a way I had not known was possible. Those experiences saved my life and gave me the foundation for doing therapy. I will always remain grateful for the experiences I had with Reich.
>
> (...) I had been a very self-conscious young man, ashamed of my background and unable to find a place in the world. Meeting Reich and becoming involved with his work changed my outlook. I had needed to build a more solid base in my personality that could support a stronger sense of self. I had needed to grow and to become more of a man. Reich had changed my life. (...) I had achieved the sexual potency that I had longed for« (pp. 42–3).

Until I read *Honoring the Body*, I never heard Al so much as hint at any shortcomings in Reich the man or the therapist. At the same time, however, he did indicate shortcomings in his own therapy with Reich: not enough character Analysis and not enough work with the deep muscular tensions. Lowen set out to develop a therapy that would take care of those shortcomings. In fact, he repeatedly acknowledges discovering that he failed to do so, and he always attributes that failure to a failure in his own development.

In *Honoring the Body* we read Lowen's account of the shortcomings in Reich's own personality and character that limited the therapy Reich was able to offer. There was not only ›the great man issue‹ and the egotistical effort to overcome humiliation on Reich's part.

> »Reich's tragedy was that he wasn't oriented toward grounding. Literally his work was toward the Cosmos. His body was heavy, puffed up, with a big chest. He was a smoker. Unfortunately, he died of a heart attack« (p. 41).

In these observations about Reich, we gain more insight into the significance and origins of Lowen's work with grounding. Bring Reich's work back to earth – Mother Earth. Further, as the euphoria he felt upon finishing his therapy with Reich declined (something experienced by many of Reich's patients), so emerged the necessity of standing on one's own two feet.

> »I realized it was one thing to feel strong and secure when one is under the guidance and protection of a powerful personality like Reich's, but quite another situation when one has to stand alone on his own two feet« (p. 43).

Once on his own, Lowen experienced within himself a loss of the sense of security and strength he had experienced while with Reich. This experience was one of the motivations for the development of his own work. In addition, I feel these significant remarks cast some light on his relationship with his father. A further consideration of his relationship with his mother will help illuminate this.

I glimpsed the force of her destructiveness to a child from a conversation with Al during a recent visit. I believe he would not mind my sharing the story. It reveals a tender and strong side of him. The story has to do with his younger sister. His mother was very destructive to her, he said. Eventually, at a time of youthful crisis, Al intervened and got her to Reich. He said that she didn't have many sessions with him, »but it was enough«, and she went on to live her life.

What was touching to me was the way he talked about his sister in the most tender, accepting, protective, and sensitive terms. I had the impression that he appreciated in her a sensitivity, vulnerability, and an unarmored state similar to a side of himself that he had to guard. He could allow in her an utter lack of worldly accomplishment that he could not allow for himself. He expressed an empathy for her that he rarely grants himself. By contrast, I sensed the way in which he has been very self-critical, very hard on himself, not just driven, but always expecting great accomplishments of himself.

In this same conversation, I asked him about his father. I gathered the same impression that is suggested in his autobiography. That after childhood, his father was hardly an influence in his life. There is no indication that he supported or was even involved in his son's development as a youth and young man.

Lowen tells us that his mother's humiliation and strange ways of relating to him bodily and sexually made him pull up. We can see, too, that his father's absence and passivity left him without the support and masculine identification that might have made him less susceptible to his mother's influence, allowing him to let back down. His therapy with Reich, he tells us, lessened his identification with his mother, but not enough. Since Reich, his therapist, hadn't resolved his own humiliation, Alexander was once again left without the necessary masculine support, just as he had been by his father.

Despite this repetition, he moved on in his life. Honesty, energy, a creative use of his mind, on the one hand, and an absence of negativity on the other, allowed him to make of his loss of his sense of security the motivation to develop the healing path he needed, using what he had acquired with Reich.

Through *Honoring the Body*, I gained a deeper appreciation and understanding of grounding and energy. I found answers to my original questions regarding Lowen's views and experiences of the mind-body split. I was particularly interested in, and learned from, what Lowen has to say in his autobiography regarding Bioenergetic therapy itself.

I will start with a striking utterance that appears to reveal a dilemma or paradox at the core of Bioenergetic therapy. »Bioenergetic therapy does not offer treatment for emotional problems« (p. 221).

This utterance shocks the mind like a zen koan. After one gets over the shock and resists the temptation not to take it seriously, I found some enlightenment. I believe he means what he says and that what he says is deeply meaningful.

He goes on to say,

> »Therapy is a self-healing process in which the therapist is a guide and facilitator. But how good a guide he is depends on his understanding of the human condition and the problems that develop when the culture, acting through the family, imposes conditions and restraints on the natural development of the human personality. Since the therapist, like every member of society has struggled with and suffered from the conflicts that arise in the interaction of culture and nature, his value as a guide depends on how much he understands the human condition and how well he has dealt with the personal traumas he has suffered growing up« (p. 221).

This passage, as I read it, is an expression of Lowen's deep faith. He has faith in the body and the healing power of the natural, energetic processes of the body. The therapist should not be ›treating‹ the patient's ›emotional problems‹, therapy in the usual sense. The therapist has a more profound task. The therapist needs to ›under-stand‹ the human condition. This is not a mental task. It means to have worked with breathing, grounding, and feeling, developing and deepening as fully as possible the pulsatory grounding wave. It means to live through whatever frightening and terrible experiences emerge and to understand them. Bioenergetic therapy is the freeing, deepening, and strengthening of that pulsatory wave. As it develops, nature takes its course and healing occurs. Nature is the Healer, not the therapist.

There is another striking aspect of this statement. Lowen did not think of himself as a revolutionary, as Reich thought of himself. However, in this passage, Lowen clearly reveals the degree to which he stands outside of culture and is a critic of culture. Just as there is a stark contrast between body and mind, so there is a stark, embattled contrast and conflict between nature and culture in the human condition.

Understanding the human condition is the understanding of the impact of culture on the biology of the organism »acting through the family«. *Fear of Life*, »my most important book«, is not primarily a discussion of the psychodynamics of the Oedipus complex. It is precisely about the impact of modern culture acting through the family on the individual. How do we understand the process of Bioenergetic therapy and the role of the therapist from these considerations? In contrast with Reich, Lowen reveals that there were several periods of crisis for him when he realized that the Bioenergetic therapy he was practicing was not bringing the desired results.

> »After working with these exercises for many years, I had to face the fact that the therapy I was doing was not really making the changes required in patients that would help them feel more fulfilled. (...) I never really failed in any situation that was important to me. (...) I became increasingly aware that I was failing in both my marriage and in my work as a therapist (p 142). (...) The issue was still grounding, but I needed a technique that would help me break through the shock state« (pp. 142–143).[2]

He is referring to 1990, age eighty. In his work as a therapist and in his work on himself, Lowen always returns to deepening grounding and the energetic pulsation. At this particular point Lowen introduced the technique of working with the golf ball and a deeper understanding of the energetic significance of the ball of the foot. His development of the grounding exercises did not end there, either.

These acknowledgments take moral courage. This is self-critical awareness. He makes it perfectly clear that he feels that the failure of his therapeutic work and of Bioenergetics generally is a direct result of his own deficiencies, and he takes full responsibility for those deficiencies, whatever their origin. It is characteristic of Lowen's style – both as a man and as a writer – that he expresses himself with simplicity, frankness, and honesty. It is not in his repertoire to try to find a more ›sophisticated‹ form of expression that will guard him against possible criticism.

The most dramatic of these acknowledgments and his most direct statement of the implications for Bioenergetic therapy is introduced with the remark, »In the course of my pursuit of pleasure, I did not see how ungrounded I had become« (p. 228). He is not talking here, of course, about sybaritic pleasures. He is referring to the pleasure he found, for example, in his Greek workshops and his becoming more widely known. »Was Bioenergetics doing the job it promised« (p. 228)? He goes on to say that the Bioenergetic exercises, as practiced in the workshops, for example, help people feel better, but they do not change character structure. Here he explicitly states what he believes the therapeutic task to be. »The therapeutic approach aims at helping a patient surrender his defensive position« (p. 229).

What follows this is a remarkable discussion of fear and death from an energetic point of view to which I commend the reader.

How is a patient to be helped in gaining the understanding of his/her fear of death that will allow him/her to relinquish the defensive position? As in all his books, in *Honoring the Body* Lowen refers to the ›two legs‹ (p. 147) of Bioenergetic Analysis, the energetic body work and the psychological work. In practice, Lowen expressed little faith in the latter as a therapeutic tool, and in his practice he focused on working with the body. Only by the fall, usually terrifying, from the ego into the body, will the individual finally be able to relinquish a defensive position. This route means accepting mortality, human limitedness, and the self as body (pp. 225, 229).

[2] See also pages 208, 210.

There is another element of therapy to which Lowen devotes attention in *Honoring the Body*. The Bioenergetic path is through the life of the body, and the life of the body is expressed in feeling. Bioenergetic exercises are meant to bring the body alive (pp. 119-20), not to make it perform or look better. Coming alive, that is working with energy, means feeling. Feelings, especially negative ones, are the basis for resistance. In addition, we fear being overwhelmed by aliveness.

Lowen mentions despair, fear, anxiety, sadness, as feelings we don't want to feel. We don't want to feel these, so we don't want to do the work and we don't want to change. »It has been hard for me to accept that most people do not want to feel more« (p. 119).

Here is how I see some of the implications of the remarks on Bioenergetic therapy. In addition to the feelings just mentioned, there are other kinds of feelings we don't want to feel. People naturally organize in defense against insecurity, humiliation, and sexual ruination, aspects of Lowen's own personality, which he shares in all humility. Deficits in the sense of self can also be experienced in even more severe forms as profound aloneness, turmoil, unreality, and a fragmented negative identity. These are not simply ›feelings‹, either. They are complex states of the self.

Feelings, in therapy, as often as not, are affective states and states of the self, body memories, and repetitions that were part of or emerged out of early relationships. Those states are very often utterly unbearable. Further, such affective states are the fuel, the motivation, and the underlying reasons for the defensive position; they drive adaptation. Giving up control and allowing the defensive position to break down as the necessary condition for allowing the free flow of energy (p. 221) requires experiencing such terrible states. Therapeutic healing means living these through with the support of the therapist, as Lowen clearly indicates, and reintegrating the emerging states as the energy is freed. Lowen mentions one such episode, remembering his experiences with his mother in his bout with enlarged prostate (p.193).

›Letting go‹ of a deep-seated adaptation which has evolved into an identity is a long, complex process. Thus, with every crisis, Lowen describes how he returned to working with his feet and grounding, each time finding a deeper experience of grounding and another useful technique for making the grounding exercises more effective. As his students we are left with this deep exploration and an understanding of the energetic processes of the body that is unique.

The way out is down, and the way down is through the pelvis, and this means there is no escape from feeling the terrible states of the self that are themselves the deepest threats to the sense of the self. »It took me fifteen more years to resolve this problem in my own personality« (p. 120), which takes him to age eighty-three.[3]

Lowen persists in his explorations and development to this day. I am grateful to this man, Alexander Lowen, for bringing his knowledge to us, and for providing a model for this kind of work, this kind of development, and this kind of therapist. What he did took courage, devotion, hard work, and continuous effort to understand. What he does, demands a confrontation with egotism. It requires an intensely devoted curiosity and motivation, and a true wish to benefit others. He brings to his mission the unusual capacity to stay the course with his own personal development for a whole, long life-time.

I am moved by the closing pages of *Honoring the Body*. The loss of Leslie naturally sent Al into deep shock. In my few conversations with him since he lost Leslie, I was struck by his awareness of the life in him. »The body has always saved me«, he says, describing how he came back to life through walking. »Feeling the flow of energy in the body is fulfillment«. He not only identifies with the aliveness, he has an utterly non-egoistic, deep sense of respect, appreciation, and even reverence for the energetic movement in his body. I understand this state as a devout appreciation of life, aliveness, and being. During this period, too, he made another exciting discovery about grounding, the exercise he calls »connecting the feet to the earth«. After that, he was equally excited about re-discovering the somersault, age 93, as a way to work with the cervical block, allowing a better connection between head and body and, thus, fuller grounding.

One image, especially, stays in my heart. It is of Al walking and »saying the word, ›Haaaa‹ «. Walking, breathing, feeling the energy in his body. Just being. I realized I was seeing a naturally religious man. He studied the nature of love, without preaching love. He described in an innovative way

---

3 See also pages 142, 208, 210.

a naturalistic meaning of spirituality without a facade of being a spiritual person.[4] He continues living his faith in life and the body. There is one other quality of a religious person he lives now.

> »One could logically and correctly define God as the spirit of the universe. (...) If we can be like God, it is in that we can partake of his nature. That nature ... is Joy« (p. 128).

I see him in this light at this stage in his life.

Reference

Lowen, A. (2004) (Ed.: Glazer, R.): Honoring the Body, The Autobiography of Alexander Lowen. Alachua, FL (Bioenergetics Press).

Philip M.Helfaer,
Ph.D., 15 Hog Hill Road,
Pepperell MA 01463, USA,
E-mail: pmhelfaer@hotmail.com

4 See pages 239, 240, 164, 239, 152, and 125–27 in that order for references in these three paragraphs.

Bioenergetic Analysis – The Clinical Journal of the International Institute for Bioenergetic Analysis (IIBA)

Editorial Office:

Dr. Margit Koemeda-Lutz
»Breitenstein«
Fruthwilerstrasse 70
CH 8272 Ermatingen
Switzerland
e-mail: koemeda@bluewin.ch

Editorial Board:

Psychosozial-Verlag, Goethestrasse 29, D-35390 Giessen.
Tel. 0049-641-77819; Fax: 0049-641-77742
e-mail: mailto:info@psychosozial-verlag.de«
http://www.psychosozial-verlag.de

Information and Instructions to Authors

1. The journal, *Bioenergetic Analysis,* publishes clinical reports, theoretical analyses, empirical investigations, and book reviews pertaining to the theory and practice of Bioenergetic Analysis.
   Articles will be published in English.
   Two reviewers will evaluate the article on the basis of a blind review (all information pertaining to the author's identity will be omitted). The Editorial Board will also have a vote regarding the appropriateness of the article for inclusion in the Journal.

2. Manuscripts should not have been published previously or been submitted elsewhere concomitantly. For manuscripts accepted for publication the copyright is automatically transferred to the publishing company »Psychosozial-Verlag« and goes back to the authors 3 month after publication.

Manuscript Submission Guidelines

3. For submission please send a disc (text as Word '98-documents, no special formats) and two printed copies of your manuscript to the Editor: Dr.Margit Koemeda, Fruthwilerstrasse 70, CH-8272 Ermatingen.
   Text can also be e-mailed (instead of sending a disk) to: koemeda@bluewin.ch« koemeda@bluewin.ch. For figures and tables we need disks.

4. Formal set-up of manuscripts
   A. 1st page:
   1)Name(s) of author(s), title of paper, address for correspondence.
   2) Summary (should not exceed half a typed page, double-spaced,
   3) Key words (max. 5)
   B. 2nd and following pages
   1) Title of the paper (without name(s) of authors)
   2) Text
   3) References

4) Footnotes
5) Tables
6) Place each table and figure with captions on a separate page, and indicate where in your text they should be inserted.
7) Include information about the author(s) on a separate page.

C. Citations and references
When citing references, include the name(s) of the author(s) and the year of publication in brackets. With more than 2 authors the first author's name and »et al.« will suffice.
Examples: Sachsse (1998) or Bacal & Newman (1994) or Streeck-Fischer et al. (2001).

D. References
All books and articles cited in the text, and only these, must be listed under »references« in alphabetical order in the following form:
Second name(s) and abbreviated Christian name(s) of all authors, year of publication in brackets, title of the publication, name of the journal, volume number, pages.
Articles from books: Second name(s) and abbreviated Christian name(s) of all authors/editor(s), year of publication in brackets, book title, publishing company, place of publication, pages.
Ex: Regli D, Bieber K, Mathier F, Grawe K (2000) Beziehungsgestaltung und Aktivierung von Ressourcen in der Anfangsphase von Therapien. Verhaltensther Verhaltensmed 21: 399–420.

Bioenergetic Analysis will be published once a year. Articles should be submitted before the end of October of the preceding year. Authors will be sent a notification of receipt of their manuscripts within two weeks and will be informed about the status of their manuscripts, (qualified) acceptance or rejection, within two months after submission.

2004 · 200 Seiten
gebunden mit Schutzumschlag
EUR (D) 19,90 · SFr 34,90
ISBN 3-89806-372-0

9/11. – Dieses Datum markiert einen tiefen Einschnitt im Selbstverständnis Amerikas und hat auch die übrige Welt erschüttert. Die Bedrohung durch den Terrorismus hat in der globalisierten Welt eine nie gekannte Dimension erreicht, und die Angst vor neuen Terroranschlägen wächst. Welche psychologischen, ökonomischen, religiösen, kulturellen und politischen Ursachen hat dieser Terrorismus? Wie funktioniert die Psyche von Selbstmordattentätern? Wie gehen die Angehörigen der Opfer mit dem erlittenen Trauma um? Welche Antworten findet Amerika auf die kollektive Demütigung? Welche psychologischen Auswirkungen haben die Terroranschläge, global gesehen? Solchen Fragen geht Hans-Jürgen Wirth in seinem einleitenden Essay nach. Er stellt Überlegungen zur psychischen Struktur der Selbstmord-Attentäter an und analysiert die psychopolitischen Ursachen und Folgen des Irak Krieges. In seinen weiteren Beiträgen geht es u. a. um Fremdenhass und Gewalt als familiäre und psychosoziale Krankheit, um das Schicksal der jüdischen Psychoanalytiker, die vor dem Nationalsozialismus nach Amerika emigrierten, und um das Menschenbild der Psychoanalyse.

2004 · 378 · Broschur
EUR (D) 29,90 · SFr 52,20
ISBN 3-89806-282-1

Terrorism, Jihad, and Sacred Vengeance delves into the psychology of terrorism and religious violence. What comprise the ideas, impulses and fantasies of terrorists and suicide bombers? How do victimization and exposure to death affect the psyche? From fascistic and paranoid responses following September 11th, 2001, to dreams of entering Paradise and blissfully joining God through acts of self-destruction, to the symbolism of evil and sacrifice, Terrorism, Jihad, and Sacred Vengeance explores the madness and despair persisting in the wake of recent events.

PSV
Psychosozial-Verlag

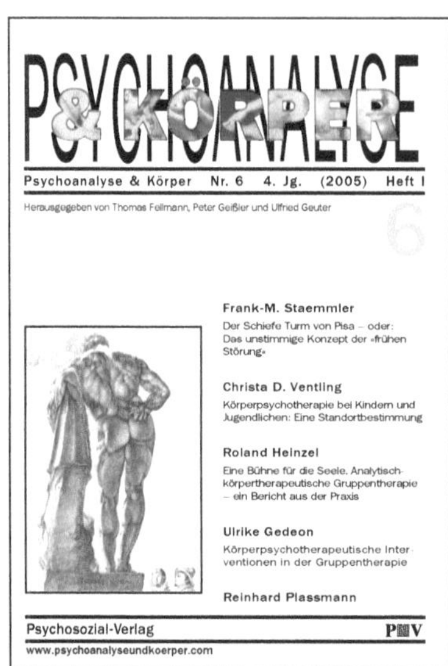

PSYCHOANALYSE & KÖRPER

Psychoanalyse & Körper Nr. 6 4. Jg. (2005) Heft I

Herausgegeben von Thomas Fellmann, Peter Geißler und Ulfried Geuter

6

Frank-M. Staemmler
Der Schiefe Turm von Pisa – oder: Das unstimmige Konzept der »frühen Störung«

Christa D. Ventling
Körperpsychotherapie bei Kindern und Jugendlichen: Eine Standortbestimmung

Roland Heinzel
Eine Bühne für die Seele. Analytisch-körpertherapeutische Gruppentherapie – ein Bericht aus der Praxis

Ulrike Gedeon
Körperpsychotherapeutische Interventionen in der Gruppentherapie

Reinhard Plassmann

Psychosozial-Verlag PSV

www.psychoanalyseundkoerper.com

Erscheint 2 x im Jahr
ca. 130 Seiten
Preis Einzelheft:
EUR (D) 14,90 · SFr 26,80
Jahresabonnement:
EUR (D) 25,– · SFr 43,80
Student/innenabo: 25 % Rabatt
ISSN 1610-5087

Eine der wichtigsten Neuerungen moderner psychoanalytischer und psychodynamischer Psychotherapie ist die Öffnung des Settings gegenüber körperbezogenen Interventionen. Auf Seiten tiefenpsychologisch fundierter Körperpsychotherapien steigt das Interesse am Beziehungsgeschehen zwischen Klient und Therapeut. Die Zeitschrift Psychoanalyse und Körper will den in Gang befindlichen Dialog durch wissenschaftliche und klinische Beiträge unterstützen und damit einen konstruktiven, Schulen übergreifenden Diskurs fördern.

PSV
Psychosozial-Verlag

www.ingramcontent.com/pod-product-compliance
Ingram Content Group UK Ltd.
Pitfield, Milton Keynes, MK11 3LW, UK
UKHW041323190726
13851UKWH00013B/74

9 783898 063951